For more than twenty years I've had the privilege of learning to lead children's ministry directly from Steve Adams. This book is not theoretical ideas. These are principles and practices I have seen Steve implement over many years of real-life, daily leadership in the local church. I am excited for you to have access to the wisdom and experience that has mentored me for so long. This is an important resource for all of us who are passionate about leading kids and families. Applying what is taught here will lead to stronger, healthier ministries.

RANDY ISOLA, Children's Pastor, Christ
Community Church, St. Charles, IL

Children's Ministry on Purpose is a book that is not just a theory or a concept on "how to"; instead we hear the heart of Steve Adams as he poses questions for us to explore. Steve is by far one of the leading children's pastors of our time, and the wisdom gained by reading this book impacts me personally, which in turn flows into my ministry. This book's layout makes thinking about your journey an easy one as you explore your world and ministry to be more purposeful, strategic, and all God intended it to be. I hope you enjoy it as much as I have!

ANDY KIRK, ACCkids National Director,
Australian Christian Churches

Having been the children's pastor for the last twenty-four years at Fellowship Church, I understand the extreme importance of being purposeful in everything I do to accomplish God's plan in the lives of the children He has given to me. However, I have found that being purposeful in children's ministry is more difficult today than ever before. In this age of quick fixes and instant impact, we've become accustomed to wanting to see the fruits of our labors immediately. Unfortunately, when working with kids, this just does not happen. When we don't see immediate results, we begin to lose focus on our end goal and wonder, "Am I really making a difference?" But this doesn't have to happen to you! Take the principles found in this book to heart and you will soon find the rejuvenation and confidence in knowing that, by developing and maintaining a long-term purpose within your ministry, you *will* be making a difference.

MIKE JOHNSON, Global Children's
Pastor, Fellowship Church, TX

Since I first heard Steve Adams share the way children's leaders should have a strategy about being intentional and balanced, my life and ministry have never been the same. His teachings can be customized to your own church and country. This book shares his love and passion for children's souls and will guide you as a leader and help you radically change your children's ministry. After reading this book, you will join this huge army of God's soldiers, as Steve says, that will change the children's landscape of eternity.

SORANLLY CAMPOS LEÓN, Children's
Ministry Pastor, Comunidad Cristiana Lirio
de los Valles, Alajuela, Costa Rica

Pastor Steve has been a mentor of mine for over a decade. He is a brilliant leader and knows how to pull the best out of people. *Children's Ministry on Purpose* takes all of his years of learning and distributes it into a book that will help children's leaders everywhere. Through his unique approach, Steve strategically leads you through a process of developing the right systems for the structure that is appropriate for your setting. It does not matter if you are full time, part time, or volunteer, this book will help you decide why you do children's ministry, define the appropriate structures, walk through how to build those structures, and determine who to get in place to make it happen! Whether you have well-defined processes and structures or if you are just starting to build them, *Children's Ministry on Purpose* will help you evaluate how you are raising a spiritually healthy generation. Together, as we continue to refine our strategies, we will become more effective in our efforts to "shape the landscape of eternity."

MICHAEL GROVE, Children's Pastor,
Calvary Church of Naperville, IL

It is not uncommon in the church world for people to stress the importance of ministry to children. However, in most churches this is the area where the highest percentage of leaders have the least amount of training and support to make it happen. In *Children's Ministry on Purpose*, Steve Adams provides some of the most foundational and practical insights to help create a structure where both spiritual and numeric growth happen while at the same time helping leaders feel more confident to fulfill their commitment to the parents, church, and children. This is by far the best book your children's leader will ever read if they want to laser focus their ministry to become everything God wants it to be.

MARK ENTZMINGER, Senior Director of Children's
Ministries, General Council of the Assemblies of God

I have worked with Steve Adams at Saddleback Church for a long time. I have often said that I have never met anybody with a better understanding of leadership and local church ministry than Steve, and that is why I am so excited about *Children's Ministry on Purpose*! This book is, without question, the best children's ministry book I have ever read, but it is much more than that. In *Children's Ministry on Purpose*, you will learn from an incredibly deep well of children's ministry, leadership, and church experience. There are lots of children's ministry books and all sorts of strategies and paradigms designed to help you do what you do a little better, but I am a believer in the strategy outlined in these pages. My own children are the byproduct of Steve's leadership and the children's ministry here at Saddleback. Also, this strategy is blatantly biblical in every area. And . . . it works! Each week, the children's ministry at Saddleback ministers to thousands of children, and churches all over the world have adapted the purpose-driven strategy in their own children's ministry with tremendous fruitfulness. Simply put, the proof is in the pudding . . . and no children's ministry is complete without a little pudding! I am so glad you purchased this book, and soon you will be too!

KURT JOHNSTON, Pastor to Students,
Saddleback Church, Lake Forest, CA

Finally! A book that shares the foundational principles of developing and sustaining a healthy children's ministry. *Children's Ministry on Purpose* is a practical and transferable tool for a church of any size, anywhere. Steve's authenticity is woven into each chapter of this book, and you will be encouraged by his heart for serving God by serving children and children's leaders!

CYNTHIA PETTY, Children's Minister,
Saddleback Church

The first time I heard Steve speak was at a conference where he laid out in a wonderfully concise way, the building blocks of an effective children's ministry. He knows what he's talking about when he talks about church and ministry. Doing tasks without purpose or intentionality is a major source of frustration and limitation in ministry. I have no doubt that this book will change the way you approach ministry to kids and provide you with a framework for "maximizing your opportunities." Read this book and discover purpose for your ministry.

DAVID WAKERLEY, Hillsong Kids
Pastor and Creative Director

CHILDREN'S MINISTRY
ON
PURPOSE

CHILDREN'S MINISTRY
ON
PURPOSE

A **PURPOSE DRIVEN** APPROACH
TO LEAD KIDS TOWARD
SPIRITUAL HEALTH

STEVE ADAMS
FOREWORD BY RICK WARREN

ZONDERVAN

Children's Ministry on Purpose
Copyright © 2017 by Steven J. Adams

This title is also available as a Zondervan ebook.

Requests for information should be addressed to:
Zondervan, *3900 Sparks Dr. SE, Grand Rapids, Michigan 49546*

ISBN 978-0-310-52301-7

Art direction: Tammy Johnson
Cover design: Lucas Design and Art
Cover photo: Masterfile
Interior design: Denise Froehlich

Printed in the United States of America

HB 12.08.2020

Contents

Foreword by Rick Warren

Many years ago when I hired Steve Adams as our Children's Pastor at Saddleback Church, I instantly knew that God was going to use him to change the face of children's ministry. Steve has an incredible heart to serve the Lord and to serve you. All of my staff pastors are committed to helping other churches develop, not just our own church. Steve's love and commitment to the church is undeniable. He is a shepherd leader who is passionate and who lives out a clear calling to raise up next-generation leaders.

There is no doubt in my mind that Steve Adams is the perfect leader to write the book on purpose driven children's ministry because he has a keen understanding that spiritual growth, just like physical growth, is a systematic and sequential *process*. Spiritual growth is not about programs. It is all about having a **biblically balanced process**.

Let me warn you. If you are looking for a book of fads, gimmicks, or quick fixes for your children's ministry, this is the wrong book. However, if you are committed to building a healthy children's ministry that lasts, this is the book for you. It is timeless. This book can show you how to build a solid, biblical, and balanced foundation for reaching and discipling children.

While this book is not an academic textbook, I feel certain that it will be used as an indispensable resource to train future children's ministers in Christian universities and Bible-training programs. I do not know of any other book like it that is based on the purposes of the church. Aligning these purposes with children's ministry has enabled Saddleback to have one of the most successful and effective children's ministries on the planet.

This book is more like a map, offering a practical step-by-step purpose driven process to discipling children. It will help you understand how to program on purpose, how to recruit and train staff and volunteers on purpose, and even how to purposefully maintain your personal life while ministering to children.

Whether you serve as a volunteer in your church, as a paid staff member, or as a parent who desires to teach kids how to move from knowing Christ to growing in Christ, to serving Christ and ultimately, to sharing Christ with others in the world—you will find all the answers here! In fact, as of 2016, Saddleback Church has sent over 25,869 adults *and children* around the world as missionaries to 197 nations!

It is a proven fact when kids grow up in an *intentional (purpose driven)* discipleship process, it is less likely that they will leave the church when they are young adults. Studies have also shown that kids who participate in a *balanced* discipleship process are those most likely to become the leaders in the church as adults. I have watched these principles used with two different generations of children at Saddleback over the past thirty-seven years. About half of my current staff grew up in our children's and student ministries, and they are solid leaders!

I urge you to study this book with others, not just read it. Get copies for those who serve in your children's ministry, and study it one chapter at a time. If you will discuss each chapter together and create a list of action steps that you intend to take, you will find all kinds of ways to implement the system that has allowed Saddleback Church to grow children to spiritual maturity.

I have been a firsthand eyewitness of how God has used Pastor Steve Adams and Saddleback's Children's Ministry to grow two generation of godly leaders. My own children, and now my grandchildren, have been powerfully shaped by this process of discipleship. I promise you that if you read this book with an open mind and with an open heart to learn from both our mistakes and our successes, and if you are courageous enough to take some risks and put these insights into practice, it will revolutionize *your* ministry to children. And that will enable you to fulfill my prayer for you, which is my life verse from Acts 13:36—that just like David did, you will *"serve God's purpose in your generation!"*

I would love to hear how this book has impacted your ministry! Write me at Rick@PastorRick.com.

DR. RICK WARREN

SENIOR PASTOR, SADDLEBACK CHURCH

Introduction: Is This Making a Difference?

Over the years, one question has echoed in the hallways of my mind, usually at the most inopportune moments. I often question my purpose and impact. I don't think I'm alone in this. And as I've talked with children's ministry leaders over the years, I've discovered that we all want to know that the time, effort, and energy we're investing actually makes a difference, that our work actually matters.

Is all of this really making any difference?

It's not easy to answer that question. When a preacher gives a message, he may receive immediate feedback from those listening, but in children's ministry, our audience doesn't usually rush up to us after a service. They don't come up to us and say, "This ministry is impacting my generation and I want to thank you for all the effort and energy you have invested in our discipleship process."

Yes, there are times when we hear a word of thanks. And sometimes the fruit of our labor is evident, but the vast majority of the time we do not see the immediate fruit. In children's ministry, there is a lot of planting and cultivating before the harvest comes. As the apostle Paul said, "I planted the seed in your hearts, and Apollos watered it, but it was God who made it grow. It's not important who does the planting, or who does the watering. What's important is that God makes the seed grow" (1 Cor. 3:6–7 NLT).

Planting seeds is more than simply placing a seed in fresh dirt and immediately tasting the fruit of your labors. It takes long, hard work. Farmers understand that when they plant a seed in the ground, there is a process that goes with the planting. The progression from planting to harvest takes time and intentionality. It requires confidence that the planting process will work. We can have that confidence because we are told that "God makes the seed grow." God has allowed us to be a part of a "seed sowing" process that has eternal implications. This is a process worth every minute of our planting efforts regardless of the demands, obstacles, and sacrifices we face. God's Word tells us that our work does make a difference.

You may be part of children's ministry because you believe in the importance of effectively discipling children. Or perhaps you're in children's ministry because you were tricked. Someone used that old "can you just fill in for a while" line, and you agreed. Regardless of why you are doing this ministry today, I believe you care about the children and this ministry or you wouldn't have picked up this book.

So why are you reading this? Most likely you love children, you want to see them grow to know Christ, and yet you worry that you aren't always effective in what you do. Or you wonder if there is a better way. So let's start with that question: Is your ministry to children effectively leading kids toward spiritual health?

Notice that I didn't ask you how many kids are in your ministry, how many volunteers you have, or whether you're happy with your curriculum. The key question we must wrestle with is whether we're effectively leading kids toward spiritual health. My goal for you in this book is to guide you on a journey of discovery. I'm not here to tell you how you should do children's ministry or to offer a "one size fits all" methodology. I want to guide you through a process of discovery that will lead to greater health in your children's ministry so your ministry will be effective in leading children toward spiritual health.

This is sometimes called a philosophy of ministry, but it is not a philosophical idea that has no bearing on reality. This process of thinking through your ministry goals and objectives will lead to practical and measurable outcomes. As you move through each chapter, you will see not only how essential this process is but you will also see how feasible and practical it is to implement. A truly healthy ministry isn't built solely on the personality of the leader or the creativity of the curriculum. It's not the result of having large numbers of volunteers. A healthy ministry that leads children toward spiritual health is the direct result of balance and intentionality in your ministry.

If you're looking for a quick fix or a resource that simply gives all the answers, this is not the book for you. This book can be a catalyst to greater effectiveness if—and only if—you're willing to invest the time and mental energy into this discovery process.

Talking about a discovery process may sound overwhelming to you. I get it. You're busy. Sunday's coming, and you're not looking for one more thing to do. But stay with me. What if in working to simply keep the ministry afloat Sunday to Sunday you are missing out on the actual point of the ministry? What if the rat race of survival mode is leading you to miss out on strategically walking kids through a discipleship process? What if you are missing entirely the main thing?

*Using a dull ax requires great strength, so sharpen the blade.
That's the value of wisdom; it helps you succeed.*

ECCLESIASTES 10:10 NLT

Sharpening Your Ax

As a boy growing up, I had the distinct "privilege" of chopping firewood for the fireplace in our home. I learned how to handle an ax and was able to get the job done quickly. But like many boys, I was impatient. I simply wanted to be done with the job so I could do what I wanted. I fell into the habit of working as hard and as fast as I could to simply get it over with and check it off my list. But as time went on, it took me longer and longer to finish the job. As the blade became duller, I found myself working harder and getting less done. One day my dad noticed how much I was straining at chopping a small load. "Son," he said," if you take care of the tool, it will take care of you." And he showed me how to "care" for the tool I was using. After we sharpened the blade, I was shocked to find that I could do the same job in half the time.

That's the question I have for you today. Will you stop long enough to sharpen your blade? I know it takes time to sharpen your tools, but there is a wonderful payoff in the end.

I'll be guiding you along this journey of discovery by asking five key questions, illustrated in this figure:

These questions will serve as a format for charting the intentional steps you need to take to ensure that you and your ministry are leading kids toward spiritual health. This discovery process also utilizes some visual components designed to help

THE FIVE KEY QUESTIONS

you develop your own unique and intentional strategy as you work with kids. Do you need to have the largest children's ministry to implement the strategies in this book? Nope. Do you need to have a big paid staff? Nope. These philosophies, principles, and concepts are being utilized by children's ministries around the world, ranging from classroom sizes of five kids to ministry centers of more than 3,500 kids. The key to this strategic discovery journey is rooted in the Bible. The foundation is biblical, the model is transferable, and the implementation is global.

The core principle of *Children's Ministry on Purpose* is derived from Rick Warren's bestselling book *The Purpose Driven Church.*[1] You will learn how a children's ministry can utilize the biblically based principles of the purpose driven approach to increase the health and effectiveness of your ministry. When I first discovered the principles in *The Purpose Driven Church* and applied them to our children's ministry, I experienced an entirely new level of effectiveness and great success.

Our church at the time was not part of the purpose driven movement. I say this because I want to be clear that you do not need to be in a purpose driven church or adopt a specific ministry model to benefit from the process I outline in this book. So don't get too caught up on the language of "purpose driven." While we use the phrase where I now serve as a pastor at Saddleback Church, what matters is not the language you use or the model you adopt—what matters is the process you walk through to develop an intentional and effective ministry plan.

The content of this book is not connected to a particular curriculum. Nor is it contingent upon subscribing to a specific methodology or theological perspective. This is a biblically rooted discovery process that will help you engage your creative side and enable you to hear from God.

My intention is not to prescribe to you how to do children's ministry; rather, my heart is to share with you a process that will lead your ministry to experience both health and effectiveness, one that has produced amazing fruit in the ministry that I've led. Only you know what your ministry really needs. You already have the ideas in your mind—they're simply waiting to be discovered!

Think of this discovery process like a lump of clay. When you initially dump the clay out of its container, you start out with a formless lump of soft clay. You roll it around in your hands, begin to mold it into cool designs, shaping it into whatever you desire. But have you noticed that the longer the clay is left out in the air, the harder it gets and the less flexible it becomes?

The development of children is similar to the shaping of clay. After a child is born and throughout his or her early elementary and preteen stages, the mind and emotions and thoughts of a child are impressionable—soft and moldable. As kids grow up, they begin to form opinions and adopt worldviews. Life experiences shape how they respond. They become less pliable, less teachable.

Am I saying that by the time they get to be adults they are

unteachable? Not at all. All I am pointing out is that change is harder as people get older. And whether you are a volunteer, a church staff member, a senior pastor, a college student, or a professor, you and I have been afforded the beautiful opportunity to invest in the spiritual health of children as they're growing. This is an opportunity to change the very landscape of eternity. So it is important that we think seriously about our own influence on the children we serve. What decisive action steps are you taking, or not taking, with your opportunity? Are you making the most of your influence?

A Few Thoughts Before We Begin

Before we get started, I want to offer a few thoughts and suggestions for using this book in a way that will lead to results.

First, process everything in stages. As you read and answer the questions, you may start to feel a bit overwhelmed. That's natural and understandable. I would encourage you to process everything in stages as you examine your ministry and ask yourself the hard questions. Utilizing the supplemental resources provided with this book will be a great help at each stage of your journey. Allow your heart to be opened to the discoveries God wants to show you. Implementing the principles in this book will require time for you to think about and do some strategic planning. But know this: you can do it.

As I mentioned before, the purpose of this book is not to present a "quick fix." Developing a healthy children's ministry takes time, patience, and a proper perspective on what's realistic. Very few things ever happen as fast as I would like them to, and the best things usually take time to develop. Remember, one step at a time in the right direction will eventually get you to your destination.

Second, recognize the value of small changes. At 211 degrees, water is really hot. If you raise the temperature of the water just one degree, to 212 degrees, something magnificent happens. The water begins to boil, producing steam, and steam produces power. What's the difference? Just one degree. In reading this book, you might discover just one principle that you can implement in your ministry. But that one principle may be the very thing God wants to communicate to you. That one principle may be the one thing that moves your ministry from 211 degrees to boiling—212 degrees.

Be encouraged and receive grace for this journey. As you read, you may come across an idea, process, or program that is used as an example and think, "I wish I could do that at my church." Don't get discouraged about what you can't do or what you aren't doing. Focus that energy on what you can do. Dream about the future and trust that God has resources you can't even imagine right now.

Write Your Own Music

A cover band is a band that plays the popular music of other bands. Cover bands are not known for the original music they have created; they are known for how closely they can copy someone else's music. If we are not careful, those of us in children's ministry can inadvertently develop "cover band" tendencies. I've done it. I would read a book or listen to a conference speaker, and I couldn't wait to get home and implement "my" new ideas. Sometimes those ideas worked, and other times they were a complete failure. We should all be willing to learn from each other and share ideas, but there is an all-too-common temptation to see what the big church is doing and assume it will work just as well for us. I'm not opposed to borrowing from others, but there is a danger. If you rely too much on the ideas of others, your church will miss out on the unique ideas God has planted in your heart for the children of your church. We should be willing to learn from each other without trying to be each other.

I have committed my life to children's ministry, and my dream has always been to make a difference. My conviction is this: Jesus was purposeful in his life and ministry, and I must be the same. I have witnessed firsthand how the principles in this book have been implemented in churches of all sizes, in many different denominations, and within different approaches to children's ministry—all over the world. Why do they work? It's simple. This approach is firmly based on Scripture and, as such, is easily transferable. Our objective as pastors and leaders within children's ministry must be to move kids toward spiritual health so that they can recognize the deception of the enemy while they embrace their true identity, purpose, and destiny in Christ. By doing so, we will change the landscape of eternity.

So, with that introduction, I want to ask, are you ready for an adventure? Are you ready to discover new pathways of effectiveness in your children's ministry? If your answer is yes, turn the page and let the adventure begin!

We've created a free discussion guide that can be used by individuals or teams for further reflection and discussion. The guide also include several exercises and activities to

help you implement the content of this book. Visit www
.childrensministryonpurpose.com to download this free
resource. In the section on "Introduction: Is This Making a
Difference?" you'll spend time discovering what your ministry really needs and taking action steps to start changing the
landscape of eternity.

CHAPTER 1

Making the Most of Your Opportunity

> So be careful how you live. Don't live like fools, but
> like those who are wise. Make the most of every
> opportunity in these evil days.

EPHESIANS 5:15–16 NLT

I'll never forget a vacation my family went on when I was eight years old. I grew up as a PK—a pastor's kid—in a church of around 130 people. Every Sunday, I was at church, sitting in the service. My dad was a good preacher, but I was a normal kid, often bored and distracted.

One weekend when my family went out of town, we ended up visiting another church. As soon as we stepped inside the front doors, I knew that this place was different. Our parents went to the adult service, and we were checked in to the kids' church, a place designed specifically for us!

We sang songs. We played games. The teacher grabbed and kept my attention. But as wonderful as all of this was, the one thing that fascinated me more than anything was the story time with the puppets. Looking back, I'm not sure why I loved the puppets, but from that moment forward, I knew I had found my calling in life. I would be the "puppet guy."

On our drive home that day, I couldn't get my ideas out fast enough. I was truly inspired, awash in creative thoughts, and I asked my dad if we could host a children's church at our church. He smiled and told me he would think about it. Several days later, I brought up the idea again and begged my dad to commission me as the puppet guy for our church. My father made a deal with me: If I earned enough money to purchase the puppets, he would build me a puppet stand and recruit an adult volunteer to help launch our own version of children's church.

I was ecstatic!

More determined than ever, I mowed lawn after lawn and earned $38. Taking my hard-earned savings to the local Christian bookstore, I bought my first puppet. My dad kept his end of the bargain. He built a first-rate puppet stand, recruited an adult volunteer, and we officially launched our first children's church. Before long, I was leading children's church—as an eight-year-old kid! I ordered the necessary materials, taught the lessons, and every Sunday I would set up the room. Years passed and I found myself in high school, yet I continued to serve in children's church. It didn't hurt that I was able to serve alongside my high school sweetheart, Stephanie, who later became my wife.

The Defining Moments in Life

That morning visiting the church was more than a fun family vacation for me. It was a defining moment in my life, one that sparked a turning point and set a trajectory for me. I share this with you because we all have defining moments. At the time, we may not recognize any one of them as a defining moment. But these significant occasions, experienced in the different seasons of life, have the potential to transform us, to launch us into a whole new realm of existence.

I've heard it said that it's not what happens in life, but how we respond to what happens that defines who we are. Or, to say it another way, it's not the circumstances, but the choices we make that determine the direction of our life. When I think about that statement, I'm reminded of other defining moments and how people responded, often in ways that would forever change the lives of generations to come. Consider Adam and Eve. Their choice altered world history forever! They chose to listen to the serpent and bite into the forbidden fruit. Or consider David and how his choice to trust God and confront Goliath changed the course of a nation. He slayed the giant with a slingshot and small stone. Or think of the impact on the course of world evangelism when Jesus appeared to Saul as he traveled on the road to Damascus. Saul became the apostle Paul and the trajectory of his life was changed forever.

Think of these life-changing moments in United States history. When John F. Kennedy declared that the United States would put a man on the moon. When Rosa Parks sat in the front of the bus rather than in the back. These moments changed our lives and we still live with the effects today. Defining moments can seem insignificant when they happen, but their effects are lasting.

Take a few moments to think about where you are today and the events or moments that brought you here. What are the defining moments in your life? Are there any that have affected your decision to be involved in children's ministry?

Defining Moments Create Opportunities

Each one of our defining moments creates a set of circumstances called an opportunity. Opportunities are gifts waiting to be unwrapped. They are the wet clay that is waiting to be shaped and molded. But the clay doesn't stay wet and moldable forever. To make the most of the opportunities we have, we must take decisive action.

The parable of the talents in Matthew 25:14–30 is a great example of this principle. It has always stood out to me because it shows what happens when we choose to act on an opportunity given to us—and what happens when we do not. In this parable, a wealthy man is preparing to leave town, and he gathers three of his servants to share with them a special assignment. He entrusts each servant with a specific sum of money to invest while he is away. To the first servant he entrusts five bags of silver, to the second he entrusts two bags of silver, and to the third he entrusts one bag of silver. The parable tells us that both the servant with five bags of silver and the servant with the two bags of silver immediately set out to invest the silver entrusted to them. The servant entrusted with one bag of silver simply dug a hole in the ground and buried the money.

When the master returned, he was pleased to discover that the first two servants, who had invested the silver, had earned double the amount of silver. But when the master learned that the third servant had done nothing with the silver given to him, he immediately took his one bag of silver and turned it over to the first servant, saying, "To those who use well what they are given, even more will be given, and they will have an abundance. But from those who do nothing, even what little they have will be taken away" (Matt. 25:29 NLT).

What was the defining moment in this parable? It came when the wealthy man gave his three servants an opportunity to build on his investments. He gave them resources to do this and encouraged them to use their creativity to take risks and grow what he had given to them. We can learn valuable lessons from this story about the opportunities God has given to us. Here are just a few to consider:

"Again, the Kingdom of Heaven can be illustrated by the story of a man going on a long trip. He called together his servants and entrusted his money to them while he was gone. He gave five bags of silver to one, two bags of silver to another, and one bag of silver to the last—dividing it in proportion to their abilities. He then left on his trip."

MATTHEW 25:14–15 NLT

First, we see that everyone is given unique opportunities. The first lesson we learn here is that wherever you are, and no matter what capacity you serve in children's ministry, you have an opportunity. These amounts weren't determined randomly or by the draw out of a hat. They were given as an intentional assessment of each servant's ability. This means that God specifically and strategically designed and gifted each of us to accomplish the assignment he has entrusted to us. Here's the awesome part: God knows what we can and can't handle. He is our Creator! He knows our limits and equips us to be who he created us to be.

Yes, the master could have divided up the bags of silver equally among the three servants. But as we see in Matthew 25:15, the master knew the ability of each of his servants, and he distributed the money accordingly. Knowing what each servant could handle, he intentionally placed each servant in the best possible scenario to succeed. He gave each servant a purpose and an opportunity. Then it was up to each servant to choose what to do.

The human body has many parts, but the many parts make up one whole body. So it is with the body of Christ.

1 CORINTHIANS 12:12 NLT

The Bible tells us that each of us is a part of the body of Christ. It takes every part, working together, for the body to function as it was designed and to truly thrive. In the same way that the wealthy man had knowledge of his servants' abilities and distributed each talent (or bag of silver) intentionally, God, in his ultimate wisdom, distributes abilities and opportunities with deliberate purpose to see us—the church body—fulfill his will. It's like what Paul said to the Corinthians: "But our bodies have many parts, and God has put each part just where he wants it" (1 Cor. 12:18 NLT). Did you catch the second half of that verse I just quoted? "And God has put each part just where he wants it." In moments when I'm tempted to think God failed in bringing the "right" opportunities my way, I must remind myself that God is a God of intentionality. He has fashioned each of us with purpose and placed us exactly where he wants us.

Consider what Isaiah tells us in Isaiah 45:9: "'What sorrow awaits those who argue with their Creator. Does a clay pot argue with its maker? Does the clay dispute with the one who shapes it, saying, "Stop, you're doing it wrong!" Does the pot exclaim, "How clumsy can you be?" How terrible it would be if a newborn baby said to its father, "Why was I born?" or if it said to its mother,

"Why did you make me this way?'" (NLT). Isaiah reminds us that God is the potter, and we are the clay. God is a beautiful, gifted, and creative artist, and he knows what he's doing. He has placed us exactly where he wants us to be.

Still, even though I know God formed me and breathed fresh life into my body, there are moments when I, the clay, like to argue with the potter. In those moments I fail to remember that since God created me, he knows me better than I know myself. I need to remember that God knows what I can handle. He created me fully knowing and understanding my gifting, my passions, and my potential.

This doesn't mean that life will be easy or that we never need to work or change. Far from it! We will constantly seek to improve, grow, change, mature, and learn new things. But we won't be as gifted in some ways as others are. There are gifts and talents I greatly admire that I don't have. There have been times when I resented the fact that I didn't have certain gifts. But I'm discovering that true joy, contentment, and fulfillment come only when I strive to be the person God destined me to be. I need to work hard to make the most of the talents God entrusted to me. Only then will I be entrusted with more.

God has given each of you a gift from his great variety of spiritual gifts. Use them well to serve one another.

(1 PETER 4:10 NLT)

Second, an opportunity lasts for only a limited time. What we learn from this story is that the master was gone for a long time. His return marked the "expiration date" for the opportunity he had given each servant. Earlier I said an opportunity is like wet clay waiting to be shaped and molded. Clay does not stay soft and moldable forever. Each servant had their chance, and the master wanted to know what each had done with the opportunity he gave them.

After a long time their master returned from his trip and called them to give an account of how they had used his money.

MATTHEW 25:19 NLT

The first two servants seized the opportunity and took action, while the third servant was paralyzed by fear and missed the opportunity. Notice the language to describe their responses:

- Servant 1—"began immediately" (TLB)
- Servant 2—"also went right to work" (TLB)
- Servant 3—"dug a hole" (TLB)

They each were working with something, and each took an action step when the master left. But only the first two took steps forward. The third stepped backward. While a defining moment will present an opportunity, you and I must take decisive action, or we will miss or squander the opportunity.

So be careful how you live. Don't live like fools, but like those who are wise. Make the most of every opportunity in these evil days.

EPHESIANS 5:15–16 NLT

Third, this parable shows us that we must see the opportunity in order to seize it. Before you can do anything with what God has given to you, you must first see it. What do I mean?

"It's right in front of you." That's what my wife, Stephanie, says when I stand at the pantry in our kitchen and ask, for what seems like the millionth time, "Where is the peanut butter?" More times than I care to admit, the peanut butter is right where she says it is, right in front of my eyes. How does that happen? Throughout my years of both seized and missed opportunities, I've discovered that the thing that most often causes me to miss an opportunity is simply a lack of awareness.

It's all too easy to miss the things that are right in front of us. It's like the farmer who wanted to sell his farm and discover diamonds in Africa. After hearing tales about other farmers doing just that, he decided to join the action. He sold his farm and set out to find diamonds for himself. And you know what? He never found a single diamond. Not one. In fact, he exhausted all of his resources. Finally, desperate and discouraged, he walked into a river and drowned.

I hear you—thanks for that depressing story, Steve. What does that have to do with defining moments, opportunities, and decisive action? Well, the story didn't end there. The man who bought the farmer's land discovered something that had been right in front of the farmer the whole time. The new land owner was walking along the creek one day and noticed something glimmering in the water. Reaching down, he picked up what he thought was a cool-looking rock. He took it home and placed it on his mantel as a decoration. One day a visitor noticed the rock on the mantel and exclaimed, "Do you have any idea what this is?" The new owner replied, "No, I have no idea, but my creek is full of rocks just like that one." The visitor, holding up the rock, said, "This is the largest diamond I have ever seen." The very thing the farmer longed for and went searching for was right in front of him all along. He already owned it! He just didn't see it. He couldn't recognize what he was looking at, and he missed it.

When I talk about the opportunity God gives us all who work in children's ministry, I call it the opportunity to "change the landscape of eternity." Picture this: You are standing in heaven looking out across the landscape. You see face after face of individuals God allowed you to influence. These people are standing there either because of the direct or indirect influence you had on their spiritual development and their decision to follow Christ. That is the landscape of eternity—a sea of individuals whose lives were touched and changed forever by Christ at work in your life.

Decisive action determines divine impact. When we make use of what we have been given, we can literally change those around us, wherever we are, forever.

To those who use well what they are given, even more will be given, and they will have an abundance. But from those who do nothing, even what little they have will be taken away.

MATTHEW 25:29 NLT

The final lesson from the parable of the talents is about faithfulness. Blessings come to those who are faithful and respond to opportunities. Did you notice that while the first two servants were given different amounts of silver to invest, they both reaped the same reward? He blessed them both with more when he discovered that they both had invested what they had been given. The master was more interested in the fact that his servants had taken decisive action with their talents, rather than the specific amount of money each made. They had done something with what they had been given.

My Calling: Another Defining Moment

That vacation visit to another church was not the only defining moment in my life. In college, I had another of those moments, one that changed the trajectory of my life yet again. In college, I did what I had always done—volunteered in my local church's children's ministry. Very soon, I was dubbed the "whatever guy." Whatever needed to be done, I did it. I cleaned classrooms, set up chairs, taught lessons, shared stories with puppets, and filled in for teachers in every age group, including the nursery! I simply showed up, received my assignment, and went to work serving kids. And I loved every second of it!

One day my senior pastor approached me with a game-changing request: "Hey, Steve, our children's pastor is no longer with us. Could you step in and fill the gap temporarily while we search for a new children's pastor? You've been serving in almost every capacity of our children's ministry, and we feel you are the right person to hold down the fort during this transition."

Without missing a beat I responded, "Sure! No problem. I'd be glad to take care of the children's ministry while you find another leader." Famous last words, right? I have a sneaking suspicion that perhaps some of you reading this may have found your way into children's ministry the same way I did . . . you were tricked into holding down the fort for "just a little while"!

Honestly, I was genuinely excited to help out during the transition. I was in my senior year of college, had recently married my high school sweetheart, and was juggling several part-time jobs. I didn't have a ton of extra time to invest in this hold-down-the-fort project, but I was going to do what I could because I loved being a part of children's ministry and wanted to support my church.

In the months that followed, I sensed a pressure I hadn't felt before. I didn't know what I was going to do with my future. Because I had been involved in church ministry for most of my life, I naturally gravitated in that direction. I assumed I would do something in youth ministry, eventually becoming an associate pastor, maybe a senior pastor—a process I was very familiar with. Being a senior pastor seemed an acceptable career path to follow. Keep in mind that this was at a time when many churches didn't have children's pastors or dedicated staff to serve children. Before going to college, I had never even heard of a "children's pastor," so that wasn't something I'd seriously considered. I struggled, wondering if children's ministry was something I could continue doing as a volunteer.

As I approached graduation, I was terrified that I would end my college career still not knowing what my next step in life should be. Each morning, I rose early to walk and talk with God. I walked all over my community and repeatedly asked God the same question, begging to discover what my next step was. I knew there was a calling on my life to lead in the local church, I just didn't know what I should lead or in what capacity. I truly wanted God's will to be done in my life. I was prepared to accept whatever he had destined for me. I remember praying this specific prayer that, in turn, resulted in another defining moment in my life.

"God, I'll do whatever you want me to do, it doesn't matter if it's full-time, part-time, or as a volunteer. I just want to know my efforts made a difference. God, how can I make the biggest difference for the kingdom?"

Over and over, morning after morning, I prayed that same prayer. More than anything, I wanted to know how I could make the biggest difference for his kingdom. I was afraid God was getting annoyed at my constant repetition. But I didn't know what else to pray. That was a large part of the reason why I said yes to lead the children's ministry as a volunteer while they searched for a new children's pastor.

One Sunday morning, as I was about to teach the lesson to the kids, God in his compassion and grace, revealed to me in dramatic fashion the answer to the question I had pestered him with for the last two months. As I began to teach, every young face in the audience grew blurry. In my mind, I heard God's voice saying these words to me: "You want to make a difference for my kingdom, then here it is." Then the blurry vision faded and the kids' faces in front of me became clear and bright.

I knew in that moment that God had created me and called me to invest my life in children's ministry. For the first time, I sensed alignment between my heart and my mind about the direction of my life and ministry. Tears filled my eyes and joy filled my heart.

That's when I realized that the kids were looking at me as if I had lost my mind.

I said nothing to my senior pastor or to any of the other volunteers. But I did share my experience with my wife, Stephanie. After several weeks, my senior pastor approached me at church one day and said, "Steve, we would like you to come on staff part-time as the interim children's pastor while we continue our search." I happily agreed, but I said nothing about the calling God had placed on my heart. After a few months in the part-time position, my senior pastor offered me the full-time role. It was just a few weeks before my college graduation. Stephanie and I prayed through the offer, and a few days later I accepted the position. And, as they say, the rest is history.

I share this with you because I think there is something very important about the question I repeatedly asked God in those years: "How can I make the biggest impact for your kingdom?" I wasn't asking God to tell me where he wanted me to go. What I wanted to know was how can I make the biggest impact for him and for his glory. And that one question launched my thoughts in a different direction. It changed my prayers and created a different level of focus for my search, guiding my heart and mind. That one question helped me discover my part in God's mission to change the landscape of eternity.

How I Make the Most of My Opportunity

Fast-forward to my sixth year in full-time children's ministry. I was serving as the children's pastor in a different church in the Midwest. I was loving my job, yet there were times when I felt as if I was going crazy. Deep down I knew something was missing. I just couldn't pinpoint what it was. I could clearly see the opportunity God had given us to influence the spiritual development of the kids in our children's ministry, but I wasn't confident that what we were doing was truly effective—at least not as effective as we could be.

That unsettled feeling led me on a quest to find out what was missing in my ministry. It turned into a third defining moment in my life—reading Rick Warren's book *The Purpose Driven Church*. Initially, when I was first handed the book, I wasn't all that interested. At that time (and similar to what we find today), new church-growth fads were surfacing every year or two. I had stopped counting the number of books I'd read that claimed to contain the way to do ministry. But the words in the title—"purpose driven"—intrigued me, and I was willing to take a peek.

I knew there had to be a more effective way to do ministry than what I was doing. I loved the kids and families in my church, and without hesitation I can tell you that my wife and I were fully committed to making a difference in their lives. The ministry was in constant motion with one event after another. We were running from one program to the next. I felt the constant pressure to increase numbers. Parent satisfaction was always a top priority.

I found myself struggling to meet everyone's expectations. I was at the point where I was willing to try anything to be able be more effective doing what I loved doing. I opened the book, and from the first page to the last, the concept of purpose driven made complete sense to me. In fact, only a few chapters into the book, I knew that my approach to ministry had to change immediately.

What changed for me? Well, before reading *The Purpose Driven Church,* I had not given serious consideration to *why* my ministry existed. I always thought that I knew why—until I tried to write it down. With the pencil hovering over the blank page, I suddenly realized it was not clear in my mind. I also became painfully aware that while my ministry was in motion and headed somewhere, I didn't know *where* it was going. I could not give a clear answer to our destination. There was a similar lack of clarity when it came to identifying our target audience. We had not established *who* we were trying to reach and, as a result, we were not being very effective in reaching anyone.

As if this was not enough, one of the biggest adjustments in my ministry came in realizing that while good things were happening, those good things were not connected to a strategy. Services, programs, and events existed in isolation and did not work together toward a specific objective. I did not have a written strategy for addressing *how* we would reach and disciple kids.

I learned that there are essential structural components that need to be in place if we are going to be successful in our mission. Knowing *what* structural components are necessary to support the ministry and then implementing those components made the difference. Now, many years later, I share this third defining moment in my life with you because I'm hoping to lead you through a similar journey of discovery. You'll have the benefit of learning from my mistakes and from the experience of others who have attempted this journey before you.

I'm not telling you how to do children's ministry. I'm providing you with an opportunity to discover for yourself the possibilities God has for your children's ministry, some of which may not have crossed your mind. I'm so confident in this process because it has worked for many people. It connects your experience, talents, and your unique opportunities to God's own leading and guidance for your children's ministry. This is an opportunity that should never be taken lightly, because it is a divine moment where kingdom possibility intersects with your own unique life purpose and gifting.

This May Be a Defining Moment for You

Think about the opportunity in front of you right now and ask yourself this question: Am I making the most of this opportunity? If not, what can I do to make the most of it? This may be a moment that changes your perspective or gets you asking different questions, empowering questions, about your future and the future of your ministry.

This might be a defining moment for you—not because you are reading this book, but because you are accepting that you have an opportunity to change the landscape of eternity right where you are. Or perhaps you recognize and embrace the fact that you are gifted by God. Or you recognize that just taking one small step, making one adjustment, can make a significant difference in your ministry to children.

Earlier, I mentioned that I often think of the spiritual development of children like forming shapes with soft clay. This time in a child's life is unique. What are you doing with the clay God has given you? What are you doing with your opportunity to make a difference in the lives of children? In the next chapter, we will begin to answer some of these questions as we explore the concept of moving kids toward spiritual health. We will also detail the essential elements for creating a ministry environment that makes the most of the opportunities in front of you.

Be sure to visit www.childrensministryonpurpose.com to download the free discussion guide. For Chapter 1 you'll spend time thinking about the defining moments of your life, the opportunities that those moments have created, and the decisive actions you must take to make the most of those opportunities.

CHAPTER 2

A Purpose Driven Children's Ministry

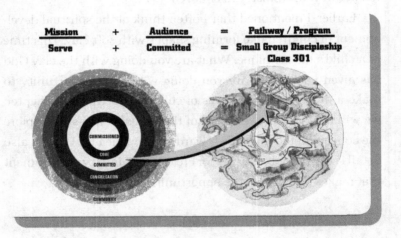

Mission	+	Audience	=	Pathway / Program
Serve	+	Committed	=	Small Group Discipleship Class 301

Don't copy the behavior and customs of this world, but let God transform you into a new person by changing the way you think. Then you will learn to know God's will for you, which is good and pleasing and perfect.

———(ROMANS 12:2 NLT)———

Put on your new nature, and be renewed as you learn to know your Creator and become like him.

———(COLOSSIANS 3:10 NLT)———

In this chapter, we'll dive into defining the nature of a purpose driven children's ministry, and you will discover how the principles I share can be implemented in your ministry. Again, I want to remind you not to become preoccupied with the language and terminology I use to describe this process. I have met some people who focus so intently on terms and specific words that they miss what really matters—the larger process that can help them reach their objective.

So with that in mind, I want to start by defining what a purpose driven children's ministry is not:

- It's not about a particular curriculum.
- It's not dependent on certain terminology.
- It's not focused on large numbers.
- It's not a "one size fits all" ministry.
- It doesn't require you to implement everything in this book.
- It doesn't claim to be *the* way to do children's ministry.

Here is how I define a purpose driven children's ministry:

A purpose driven children's ministry is an
intentional and balanced discipleship process
that leads kids toward spiritual health.

There are four key components to this definition, and each of these will be covered in this book:

1. Spiritual Health
2. Balance
3. Intentionality
4. A Discipleship Process

There are two features of my definition that warrant a closer look. Let's unpack what it means to say we are "leading kids" and what we mean by "spiritual health."

Leading Kids

Leadership is an art of influencing people to follow you to a destination. I say that we are leading kids not to imply a position of power and authority, but to suggest that we are guiding children along their journey—not pushing or pulling them. While we have a clear objective and a specific destination, each child is unique, and their journey will reflect that uniqueness. Children will have questions and experience doubts at each stage of their spiritual development, and it's important to help kids navigate those questions and doubts as they grow and mature. As we lead them, we want them to know and understand God's Word, but also to discover how to live out their faith in every arena of their life.

The apostle Paul was leading a group of believers (that sometimes acted like children) on a journey toward spiritual health. He gave them a message in Philippians 3:16 that beautifully describes the discipleship process: "Only let us live up to what we have already attained."

Paul knew that these believers were at different stages in their spiritual formation, and he wanted them to understand the importance of acting on the guidance they each had received by this point along their individual journeys. In other words, they could not progress in their spiritual health development until they understood and faithfully implemented the truth they already knew.

Paul led them toward spiritual health and maturity, but it

was up to the individual to learn and live the truth that Paul taught and exemplified.

We lead kids in the same way. We guide them along a spiritual formation journey by teaching them the Word of God and helping them to navigate honest questions as they process personal doubts and discover how to make it through confusing and discouraging times. As they genuinely act on the truth they have learned, they progress one step at a time in their journey toward spiritual health and becoming a disciple of Christ.

Spiritual Health Is the Goal

We are leading kids to a destination, and that destination, or goal, is spiritual health. This requires a process of balance and intentionality. The beauty of this journey of spiritual formation is that it culminates in life transformation, which is the pathway to spiritual health. This does not happen by the mere transfer of information or a "believe it because we said it" approach. It is a journey with highly committed Christ followers guiding the kids, one step at a time, along the way.

The vast majority of the time when we think of the word "health" we immediately envision the human body—and rightly so. It's an organic image of wholeness and well-being. Throughout the Bible we see the human body used as an illustrative tool to help us understand principles and truths, such as unity in the church, the interrelationship of believers, and the necessity of diversity in gifts and talents.

The human body also illustrates a profound picture of spiritual health. When the systems, parts, and processes of the human body operate in balance according to God's masterful engineering, your body will develop and function as it was designed. This is generally regarded as health. We innately assume that a healthy body is a body functioning at its optimal level.

However, we all face ongoing challenges with our physical health. This may be due to a birth defect, an injury, a hereditary disorder, poor choices, or even the natural process of aging. Do these challenges necessarily prohibit us from being healthy? For example, if I am missing a limb, does that mean I can never be healthy? Or if I have a mental illness, does that mean I am forever excluded from the "healthy party"? Even when my body systems aren't functioning properly or all of the chemicals aren't balanced perfectly, that doesn't mean that a level of health is out of reach for me. Honestly, I don't know many people who have perfectly healthy bodies free from any imperfection or limitation.

This suggests that physical health will not look the same for everyone. Our bodies all have the same ideal design, but because of a variety of reasons, our bodies function differently. Some people have achieved a level of health in their physical bodies that is not possible for me. That doesn't mean I can't be healthy; it just means we can't define healthy with one broad stroke. A body that is functioning at its own optimum physical level and reaching its full potential is healthy.

I believe the same is true of our spiritual health. We each have obstacles, struggles, and limitations. Some are the result of our choices; others are the result of matters outside of our control. But no matter what the obstacle is or how it originated, we can be spiritually healthy even if spiritual health looks different for each one of us. Spiritual health is the progressive process of a person reaching their full potential in their growth and development as a disciple of Christ.

We're all somewhere along our journey toward spiritual health, a journey to becoming spiritually mature. We all need guidance, especially those who are young in the faith. Improvements in spiritual health will not happen without deliberate effort by the disciple, however young they are, and by the leader guiding them. Paul, on various occasions, used the analogy of growing toward maturity, as when he wrote to the Ephesian church: "This will continue until we all come to such unity in our faith and knowledge of God's Son that we will be mature in the Lord, measuring up to the full and complete standard of Christ" (Eph. 4:13 NLT). Paul is reminding the church that spiritual health is not a gift for the few; it's a gift for all of us. In fact, we cannot achieve spiritual maturity on our own. We achieve it corporately as we grow together as Christ's body. But getting there requires a deliberate commitment to grow "in every way more and more like Christ" (Eph. 4:15 NLT).

As we discover and develop spiritual formation steps that lead kids toward spiritual health, we must remember that each child is unique. They are at different life stages, with different backgrounds and different levels of potential. No matter where they are in their journey, every child has the potential to be spiritually healthy and to continue moving toward the next stage of spiritual health.

A Healthy Ministry Leads Kids toward Spiritual Health

Just as the human body can be an illustration of our spiritual health, it also can help us to understand how we can have a healthy ministry. Your ministry in the church, much like the human body, is a living organism that requires essential processes, systems, and structures to sustain health. And just like the human body, when your ministry is healthy, it grows, develops, and functions according to its unique potential. Paul said in Colossians 2:19: "It is from [Christ] that all the parts of the body are cared for and held together. So it grows in the way God wants it to grow" (NCV).

The growth of your ministry is not as important as the health of your ministry. Our responsibility is not to manufacture growth, but to take the necessary steps to provide a healthy environment. God will make the ministry grow according to his plan. It is for this reason that you cannot judge the health of a ministry on numbers alone. If numbers become the focus of your ministry, you will lose sight of the primary objective, which is health.

While I believe it's important to track and gauge metrics, such as attendance and growth, I don't believe the number of kids involved in a ministry is an accurate barometer of the health of a ministry. This is also true with regard to the spiritual health of the kids who attend a ministry. While it is tempting to track numbers—attendance, the number of Bible verses memorized—I have found it incredibly difficult to measure the spiritual health or spiritual maturity of a child based solely on their level of involvement in our children's ministry.

The Bible says in Matthew 7:15–20 that we can identify a tree by its fruit, but as you probably have experienced, sometimes the fruit isn't exactly what you thought it would be. I'm reminded of the avocado tree in my backyard. Anyone who looks at that tree knows it's not an orange tree or an apple tree. It's an avocado tree. Avocados grow on it. But not every avocado is the same quality of fruit. I have cut into one of those beautifully green and ripe avocados only to discover that it's not as ripe and nice on the inside as it looks on the outside. The same is true with the "fruit" produced by our ministry. Yes, attendance and memorized verse numbers are nice and can be signs of a healthy ministry, but they aren't a guarantee. The fruit may not be ripe. It might even be unhealthy or have a disease.

By striving for health, your ministry has an opportunity to reach its full potential and grow in the way God wants it to grow. The essential processes, systems, and structures necessary to provide a healthy ministry environment require a coordinated effort by individuals committed to doing their part. The apostle Paul describes the goal we are seeking in ministry health in the book of Ephesians when he says that Jesus "makes the whole body fit together perfectly. As each part does its own special work, it helps the other parts grow, so that the whole body is healthy and growing and full of love" (Eph. 4:16 NLT). The two key elements to have and sustain health in your ministry are balance and intentionality. Let's take a closer look at these key elements and discover how to implement them in our ministries.

Balance Is Essential for a Healthy Ministry

As we saw earlier, health does not mean perfection. No matter how purpose driven your ministry is, imperfections are bound to emerge. The goal for leaders is to develop and operate to your own full potential, and this requires balance.

Can you imagine walking on a thin wire stretched between two buildings that are more than a hundred stories from the ground? Or walking on a wire across Niagara Falls? How about walking on a tightrope stretched between two Swiss mountain-tops? Sounds a little crazy, right? But each of these events did take place. I get queasy just thinking about it.

What do you think these tightrope walkers were focusing on as they crossed the divide? Balance. Without proper balance, they would have fallen to their death. To take each next step, they had to focus on maintaining their balance. Balance is the key to a successful tightrope walk.

Balance also is key in many areas of life. We underestimate the importance of balance the longer we walk in a particular direction or do a particular task. We develop tunnel vision, which leads us to neglect important parts of our lives.

Our ministry to children is no different. If we want to experience true health and make the most of every opportunity in front of us, we must seek balance. In *The Purpose Driven Church*, Rick Warren says this about balance: "There is no single key to church health and church growth; there are many keys. The church is not called to do one thing; it's called to do many things. That's why balance is so important." As Paul points out so vividly in 1 Corinthians 12:12–31, the body of Christ has many parts. Our human body is not comprised of just a hand or a mouth or an eye. It is made up of multiple interworking systems—the respiratory system, the circulatory system, nervous system, digestive system, skeletal system, and so forth. When these systems are in balance with each other we say the body is healthy. When we're imbalanced, it's called illness. So what does a balanced spiritual "body" look like? It's a body that incorporates each of the major New Testament purposes of the church. In purpose driven language, these are five major purposes God has for the church:

1. Worship
2. Belong
3. Grow
4. Serve
5. Share

Together, these purposes come together to create the framework for a healthy environment, one poised to reach its full potential in leading kids toward spiritual health. At Saddleback Church we call this being "purpose driven," but again, don't get stuck on that phrase. You may call it something else. The bottom line is that God has given us in his Word a beautiful picture of balance—incorporating the different purposes, or systems, of a healthy church into a unified whole. These can be replicated in any ministry environment. Being purpose driven is simply a matter of being purposeful in ministry by creating the right conditions for spiritual health through balance.

And that brings us to the second point. Achieving the necessary balance for health will not happen automatically. You must be intentional.

You Must Be Intentional to Create Balance

When my sons where younger, we spent a fair amount of time playing with LEGOs, those small plastic bricks that come in various shapes and sizes. While I'm sure there are some limitations to what a LEGO set can do, I haven't found them yet.

As the years went by, we expanded our collection of LEGOs to the point where we each had enough to build whatever we imagined. We would simply empty the container of LEGOs on the floor and start putting them together. Once those colorful bricks covered every square inch of the carpet, the boys and I would dive into the pile like a pack of hungry dogs. Sometimes we would have a predetermined plan, but most of the time we just slapped pieces together, taking no special care or attention to what we were actually making. We made it up as we went along and had no concept of the end result we were moving toward. We waited for chaos to magically transform into order. Unfortunately, that order never happened. Our creations were interesting, but they didn't have a clear design or purpose to them.

A few years later, we were introduced to a new type of LEGO—a LEGO kit with specific pieces predesigned to build a very specific structure. By following the instructions, anyone could make a robot, a race car, a jet airplane. Our method of throwing out pieces and slapping them together wouldn't work to create these masterpieces. To build these structures, the assembler had to follow the instructions step by step.

When we sat on the floor and put pieces together randomly, we didn't know how it would turn out. A wall might turn into a bridge, which might turn into a boat. And if you looked closely at the "boat," you probably would not recognize it as a boat. We had good intentions, but without a design and a plan, you probably would not be able to tell what we were making. One time I remember my son Matt putting some LEGOs together to make a spacecraft and saying, "Look, Mom!" Stephanie responded, "Oh, you made a little house!" Disappointed, Matt replied, "No, it's a spaceship." Matt knew in his mind what he wanted to make, but the result was not recognizable to anyone else.

I share this because the same is often true in our ministry. When the ministry is randomly assembled, I may think it is one thing, but it might look like something else to other people.

A ministry that is intentional has a deliberate approach with predetermined outcomes. In a world that offers an endless supply of random activities, distractions, and deceptions, ministry leaders must be focused and on point about the goals of their ministry. God is a God of order, not chaos. He has purpose and intention in what he designs. Look closely at any creation in nature, and you will quickly recognize cohesive patterns. Our God, the Creator of the universe, builds with purpose and intention, all while keeping his perfect eye on the desired outcome. Friends, we are made in his image, and we should do our best to follow his example.

Jesus was intentional in equipping his disciples. He intentionally selected each disciple, deliberately teaching them lessons and consciously assigning tasks designed to accomplish a predetermined outcome. We too should approach ministry with intentionality and leave the randomness to our living room LEGOs. At its core, a "purpose driven" children's ministry is intentionally structured to maximize the potential God has for his church.

We need balance and intentionality. To maintain balance, we must set up both a system of processes and a structure of strength and support to intentionally balance the five purposes of God. If we don't do this, we will follow our natural tendency to emphasize what we feel most strongly about and neglect whatever we feel less passionate about. The result may well be missing the proper intentionality and balance.

A Purpose Driven Children's Ministry Is a Discipleship Process

Earlier in this chapter we defined a "purpose driven children's ministry." Did you catch the words "discipleship process" in that definition? Here's the definition again:

> A purpose driven children's ministry is an
> intentionally balanced discipleship process
> that leads kids toward spiritual health.

Those two key words, *discipleship* and *process*, are important for us to understand. Let's start with the word *disciple*. What does it mean to be a disciple? The word *disciple* refers to an apprentice or a student. In Jesus' day, a disciple or student would literally follow his teacher everywhere he went. The disciple would listen carefully to the instructions and teachings of the teacher (or rabbi) and would commit themselves to becoming like that teacher. The goal wasn't just learning information, but experiencing life transformation. This experience of being a disciple requires action. It requires more than simply understanding facts or making a halfhearted attempt and giving up. Becoming a disciple means focusing on the goal of becoming like our teacher, living as he lives. Like Jesus said, "Students are not greater than their teacher. But the student who is fully trained will become like the teacher" (Luke 6:40 NLT).

In Jesus' time, becoming "like the teacher" was the goal of being a disciple or student. During the process, the student was exposed to the instruction of the teacher, listened as the teachings were explained, experienced the reality of those truths, and then was given the opportunity to express what he had learned by sharing it with others. Today we might add that a student is not only a learner. A student is also a practitioner—putting into practice the things they learned. Philippians 3:16 is helpful here: "Only let us live up to what we have already attained." To become like our teacher, we must also obey, or put into action, what we learn.

In *The Purpose Driven Life*, Rick Warren describes a disciple as one who:

> Is pleasing God every day, this is WORSHIP.
> We are planned for God's pleasure.

Has joined a fellowship of believers, this is FELLOWSHIP.

We are formed for a family.

Is learning to be more Christlike every day, this is DISCIPLESHIP.

We are created to become like Christ.

Is serving in ministry in their church, this is MINISTRY.

We are shaped for service.

Is sharing God's love with unbelievers, this is MISSION.

We are made for a mission.

Francis Chan addresses this concept of being a disciple as becoming like the teacher. In his book *Multiply* he writes: "That's the whole point of being a disciple of Jesus: we imitate Him, carry on His ministry, and become like Him in the process. Yet somehow many have come to believe that a person can be a 'Christian' without being like Christ. A 'follower' who doesn't follow. How does that make any sense? Many people in the church have decided to take on the name of Christ and nothing else."[2]

Some also use the words "spiritual formation" to describe what I am referring to as the "discipleship process." Rather than get into the weeds about which language to use (there are other books on that), I will note that some church leaders use these terms interchangeably while others have made a case for preferring one over the other. For the purposes of this book, I will use the terms "discipleship process" and "spiritual formation" to mean the same thing. They are just different ways of stating what it means to become like Christ.

In his book *The Great Omission*, Dallas Willard said this about spiritual formation: "What we must understand is that spiritual formation is a process that involves the transformation of the whole person, and that the whole person must be active with Christ in the work of spiritual formation. Spiritual formation into Christlikeness is not going to happen to us unless we act."[3]

So how does this work in a children's ministry? Here is a quick explanation of what it looks like in our children's ministry at Saddleback. In a discipleship process, a Christ follower is progressively becoming more like Christ through transformation. Spiritual formation is the framework we use to help kids know and grow in their relationship with God through the process. We use spiritual formation as a means of helping the kids become disciples of Christ.

We promote a systematic approach that moves kids from being unchurched and unconnected to God to a deeper level of spiritual maturity and commitment, where they are involved in ministry and living out their God-shaped mission in the world. This is more than just the mere transfer of information from a teacher to a child; it's a transformative process by which the living God is made real and approachable to children. It's what Paul said in his letter to the Romans: "Don't copy the behavior and customs of this world, but let God *transform* you into a new person by *changing* the way you think. Then you will learn to know God's will for you, which is good and pleasing and perfect" (Rom. 12:2 NLT, emphasis mine).

The word "transform" in this verse appears again in Matthew 17 when Jesus takes Peter, James, and John up a mountain to pray. The usage is helpful for understanding the meaning of Paul's message. When Jesus and the disciples get to a certain place on the mountain, something miraculous happens: To the disciples' amazement, right before their eyes, while praying, Jesus' personal appearance is transformed into a glorified form. His face shines brightly like the sun, his clothes become dazzling white, and Moses and Elijah appear before them. They even have a conversation with Jesus. Can you imagine what Peter, James, and John were thinking in this moment? I would have been scared to death!

Have you ever wondered why Jesus did this? I think one of the reasons why Jesus allowed Peter, James, and John to witness this moment was to provide those closest to him with a greater understanding of who he is. Until this moment, the disciples only knew Jesus in his human form and identity. But when Jesus' appearance dramatically transformed, the disciples could see Jesus in all his glory. Even though they could not completely comprehend what had just transpired before their eyes, they walked away from that experience with a greater realization that Jesus was more than just a man. They began to grasp more of the deity of Christ as well.

The reason I mention the transfiguration of Jesus in Matthew 17 is to point out that the same word used in Romans 12 for "transform" is used for "transfiguration" here: the word *metamorphoo*. Just as God transformed Jesus' appearance into something amazing, God wants to do the same in us. This isn't just a slight improvement—it's an entire makeover! God wants to turn us into people who display his glory. While our faces might not literally shine like that of Jesus, God wants our lives—our hearts, thoughts, actions, words, and deeds—to clearly shine and tell others that something has happened to us. And this is what God wants for the kids within our sphere of influence— transformation along their journey toward spiritual health.

In chapter 1, I mentioned how I often think of the children in our ministry like clay. Our kids will be shaped and molded, but the question we should ask is by whom and toward what end? This pliability and receptivity we find in children grows less flexible each year. That is why I firmly believe that the maturity and spiritual health children gain at a young age through an intentional discipleship process will prepare them to fulfill their God-given purpose, embrace their true identity in Christ, and take hold of their unique calling in this world.

Jesus effectively modeled a transformative discipleship process. Jesus had only a short amount of time—about three years—to prepare his disciples to carry out the mission of sharing God's love with the world. Think about that—he had three years to equip, encourage, and empower his team of future leaders. In those three years, two aspects of Jesus' discipleship process stand out as necessary for us today if we want to maximize our effectiveness in seeing children's lives transformed. Jesus' discipleship process was strategic and developmental.

A Strategic Discipleship Process

Years ago it was not uncommon for my ministry to offer a wide variety of events and programs. Each of these events and programs were good and everyone seemed to approve—well, at least most of the time. But there was a problem: The events and programs were isolated and not connected to each other. We didn't have a strategic process to prioritize or integrate them, and this meant that I wasn't maximizing our efforts or resources. All of the "good things" we were doing were scattered and less effective because they weren't supporting or building upon each other. Our events and programs were disconnected. Rather than a synchronized ministry that takes kids through a discipleship process, we found ourselves spinning our wheels.

That's why our kids weren't getting anywhere. We weren't strategically aligned.

A few days after we talked about this problem, I was reading a magazine and saw an advertisement for a nice handcrafted wristwatch. The watch was beautifully designed with a price tag that matched. But what caught my eye was an illustration called an "exploded view." This illustration revealed all the parts of the watch as if the watch had just exploded. It allowed me to see the inner workings in a creative manner. A light bulb went off in my head.

I saw that all of the uniquely shaped parts of that watch worked together with one singular objective: to accurately keep time. There were many moving parts, but they had a united purpose. In the same way, our children's ministry has a number of "moving parts." But we must ask ourselves, Are those moving parts aligned and functioning together to achieve a strategic objective? Like a purposefully crafted mechanical clock, purpose driven children's ministries are strategically designed toward a singular objective: to move children toward spiritual health. This is what it means to be strategic. A strategic ministry takes into consideration all the factors necessary to achieve a predetermined goal and examines how those factors are connected to each other.

If you serve in children's ministry, you know that there are many aspects of the ministry that people outside aren't aware of. Most people don't know what you as the children's ministry leader must do each week just to keep the ministry going—until you don't do it. Like a mechanical clock, each part or component of our ministry should be connected and built together as a whole, all while working toward a common objective. Jesus was extremely strategic in every aspect of his ministry. He knew what had to be accomplished, how it would be accomplished, and who he needed to accomplish the objectives. Jesus looked at his ministry from a big-picture perspective. Understanding that not everything could be done at once, he strategically thought through step by step how he would disciple these leaders and how he would utilize each of their skill sets for kingdom purposes. Doing so also meant he pulled from unlikely sources. Those he chose to disciple were not always the crowd favorites or ones we might have voted for, but he knew precisely who could accomplish each task and how they fit into the larger picture.

A purposeful children's ministry maximizes its effectiveness and makes the most of every opportunity through strategic thinking—like clockwork!

A Developmental Discipleship Process

The discipleship process happens in steps and stages, not all at once. I add "developmental" here because the strategy must be designed to connect with kids on their developmental or spiritual level. Consider an analogy from grade school. We teach our kids the principles of mathematics through a developmental process. First, kids learn to identify numbers, then they move on to addition and subtraction, then to multiplication and division, and finally on to the truly fun aspects of mathematics—algebra, trigonometry, and calculus!

Now imagine for a second if we switched the process and began teaching calculus to first graders before they had learned or mastered multiplication and division. This is a crazy idea, right? We must take kids on a developmental journey through the different fields of mathematics, each stage building upon the one before it. Progress is both incremental and cumulative, developing in stages. In this sense, it's like learning to walk. Children must learn to crawl before they can walk. They call them baby steps for a reason.

Jesus modeled a developmental approach with his disciples. Initially, Jesus framed his teaching with "come and . . . see" (John 1:39). From there he taught them in stages and steps what it meant to be a disciple. As their understanding grew and matured, the framework moved from "come and see" to "come and die."

In Matthew 4:19, Jesus approached Peter and James and challenged them to follow him: "I will show you how to fish for people!" (NLT). It was an invitation to influence the eternal and their opportunity to change the landscape of eternity. Then, as his mission was coming to an end and not long before Jesus was to be crucified, he gave his disciples a new challenge: "If any of you wants to be my follower, you must give up your own way, take up your cross, and follow me" (Matt. 16:24 NLT). The disciples knew what that meant. Three years earlier the call to die probably would have been too much for them, but after three years of transformative experiences, they not only understood what Jesus was asking, they were prepared to follow Jesus' example and commission (see John 11:16; 13:37; Matt. 26:35).

Jesus used a developmental strategy (even if he didn't use those words) by incrementally teaching and modeling in different stages according to the disciples' needs and progress. Like the disciples, our children will progressively move from knowledge and experience to full devotion—from "come and see" to "come and die." That's the goal.

Christian brothers, I could not speak to you as to full-grown Christians. I spoke to you as men who have not obeyed the things you have been taught. I spoke to you as if you were baby Christians. My teaching was as if I were giving you milk to drink. I could not give you meat because you were not ready for it. Even yet you are not able to have anything but milk.

1 CORINTHIANS 3:1–2 NLV

The apostle Paul told the people in Corinth that he was unable to speak with them the way he wanted because they were not yet spiritually mature enough. Paul had to address or approach them "where they were" in their spiritual journey.

Good storytelling, engaging object lessons, and fun games are great ways to connect with kids, but these things lose their impact without an intentional process that strategically and developmentally moves kids toward spiritual health. When we have both of these elements, we will maximize our effectiveness with kids.

A Purpose Driven Discipleship Process Maximizes Effectiveness

In children's ministry, we have only a short amount of time to lay a foundation for spiritual formation. A strategic and developmental discipleship process will maximize your effectiveness in four vital ways to help you achieve your goal of leading children toward spiritual growth.

First, this process will give you a clear picture of the discipleship opportunities your ministry currently provides. When we start with the end in mind, we are able to identify different pathways that will guide kids toward the ultimate objective—spiritual health. Our effectiveness is maximized when we know where we are leading kids and how we are leading them.

Second, this process helps you properly allocate resources. How we utilize resources entrusted to us can make or break how effective we are in ministry. Knowing where we spend our time, effort, and energy allows us to identify how we're leading children toward spiritual health and to make necessary adjustments to maximize our effectiveness.

Third, this process shows you how each component of your ministry is working together toward the objective of spiritual health. Here's our mechanical clock again—the whole is only as effective as the sum total of how the parts work together. When we clearly identify how each component of our ministry works (or does not work) together, we can assess how well we are reaching our objective and make the necessary strategic adjustments.

Finally, the process helps you to ask the right questions and find the right solutions. It's easy to get stuck in "problem-solving mode" as children's ministry leaders. However, we find solutions by asking the right questions. The questions we ask determine which direction our thinking goes. I like this quote from Voltaire, "Judge a man by his questions, rather than his answers."

When we ask the right questions, we direct our minds toward the right answers. But it is all too common to get stuck on the wrong trajectory by asking the wrong questions. Have you ever found yourself stuck asking the following questions?

- How can I get more volunteers?
- What curriculum should I use?
- Why doesn't our senior pastor care about children's ministry?

- Why are kids so disruptive, and why do they misbehave every week?

I've been there. These questions have their place, of course. But they are shortsighted, and the answers you find will give you only temporary relief from the deeper challenges you face in your ministry.

Whatever you are looking for you will eventually find if you seek it with all your heart. That's the way the kingdom of God works (John 15:7; Jer. 29:13). Let's say you have a difficult child in one of your elementary classes (one of the "extra grace required" kids). No matter what you do, you can't keep the child's attention. The child is a constant disruption, will not sit still, and gets into everything. When you are in your car driving home from service, you might ask yourself, "Why is Steve such a bad kid?" Your brain immediately goes on a search to find all the potential reasons why Steve seems like a bad kid. Soon you begin to see every little "bad thing" Steve does. Why? Because your mind, whether you are conscious of it or not, is focused on finding the answer to your question. If you have already determined that Steve is bad, there are a limited number of directions your mind can go to uncover the solution to your problem.

But let's see what a different approach looks like. We start with the same situation with our "extra grace required" child. Only this time on the way home you ask yourself this question, "What could I do to get Steve engaged so he will connect more with the lesson?" Now your brain is searching for ways to help Steve connect with the teaching. Do you see the difference?

And by the way, if it encourages you that children can change, I should mention that I was that kid. I'm a constant reminder to myself of why we don't give up on the "problem kid." Because one day you might find yourself reading one of his books (wink, wink).

Over several decades in children's ministry, I have learned that we must ask better questions if we want to find the right answers. Great thinking begins with great questions. So let's reframe the earlier questions to see how better questions direct our thinking to better solutions:

- Why are volunteers not lining up to serve in our children's ministry?
- What do our kids need to know in order to grow in their relationship with Christ?
- What can we do to show our senior pastor that our children's ministry is in line with his vision for the church?
- What could I do this week to more effectively connect with our kids?

The difference between these questions and the previous ones is that these questions energize instead of overwhelm, they inspire instead of overshadow feelings of defeat, they create anticipation instead of feelings of dread, and they open doors of creativity that may have otherwise remained closed. Jonas Salk said, "Find the right questions. You don't invent the answers, you reveal the answers." Our questions drive our thoughts, and our thoughts drive our actions.

Now Steve, you may be saying, I am far too busy to stop what I am doing to reflect on asking better questions. The weekend service is quickly approaching, and someone's got to make sure it actually happens! Let me say that I completely understand where you are coming from. I have been in your shoes for the majority of my years in ministry. However, I'd like to challenge you to consider what Bob Rosen says in his book *Grounded*. Many leaders, he says, "cling to old mindsets and accept outmoded ways of thinking. Primary among their misconceptions is focusing too much on action and too little on introspection."[4] I understand that programs need to be maintained. But at some point, you will need to set aside time to think and reflect. And one of the best places to begin is to examine the questions you are asking yourself and the others in the ministry. An effective children's ministry that leads kids toward spiritual health starts with asking the right questions.

So as we begin this process of reflection, we will ask a few questions. I suggest starting with the first of the five key questions we will address in this book: Why?

The question of why will serve as the catalyst for your ministry going forward. Your answer to the why question will become the foundation for your ministry and will provide you clarity for the difficult times.

Visit www.childrensministryonpurpose.com to download the free discussion guide with reflection questions and activities for Chapter 2. You will begin to reflect on the importance of spiritual health and balance in your ministry and talk about how the discipleship process maximizes effectiveness.

CHAPTER 3

Why Does Your Ministry Exist?

Many are the plans in a person's heart, but it is the Lord's purpose that prevails.

PROVERBS 19:21

Children are natural-born questioners. If you've spent more than thirty seconds with a child, you know! Kids are full of questions. Some are intriguing, many are embarrassing, and some are downright annoying.

What is the question children most often ask? You guessed it—why?

Children are curious. Their incessant and relentless "need to know" drives them to ask anything that comes to mind. Sometimes this can be really funny! Over the years I've heard some great ones, like "Did Jesus use the potty? Why does that lady have a moustache? Why do you have to go to work every day? Why do you have spots on your face? Do you have to put them on every day? Why do vegetables have to taste so bad?"

Sometimes children ask why because they don't understand or like a directive they have been given. You've asked them to do something and they don't want to do it. So they ask why? Countless times, when my wife, Stephanie, and I have told our sons, Tyler and Matt, to do something, their response has been the same: Why? Why do I have to do my homework now? Why do I have to make my bed? Why can't I watch this show? Why, why, why? As parents, this question can drive us nuts. In those moments, when it's not convenient to give a long and detailed explanation, we use the one answer we said we would never use: "Because I said so." It's quick and easy to appeal to your authority as a parent. The challenge is that as children grow older, that authority isn't as compelling to them. That's why it's important to provide a real answer instead of pulling rank.

Kids aren't the only ones who ask why. Everyone asks that question on some level. We have parents and other leaders asking why, and it's important to clearly explain our reasoning. As we work with parents, leaders, or a team of volunteers, sometimes we need to answer their why questions even when it's difficult to explain. But adults are no different than kids in this regard. When we are given a directive we don't understand or don't like, just like the kids, we want to know why.

But that's not the only reason we need to answer the why question. Knowing why motivates us. It's always easier to put your whole heart into something when you truly know why you are doing it. Friedrich Nietzsche once said, "He who has a why to live for can bear almost any how." Unfortunately, as we grow older, we start to realize that asking questions can create trouble, and we decide it's better to just "go with the flow" and not cause any waves by asking questions. Over time we begin to lose that curiosity so common in children. Have you ever noticed that children can ask almost anything and get away with it, but as an adult, asking questions is viewed negatively.

It's time for us to start acting like children again. I am not advocating that we eat Play-Doh or draw on walls with crayons. But we must get back to asking questions. Not random, meaningless questions. We must start asking the good questions, the empowering questions. I love how E. E. Cummings so eloquently stated this: "Always the beautiful answer who asks a more beautiful question." Asking good questions leads to great discoveries.

Albert Einstein once wrote, "The important thing is not to stop questioning. Curiosity has its own reason for existing. One cannot help but be in awe when he contemplates the mysteries of eternity, of life, of the marvelous structure of reality. It is enough if one tries merely to comprehend a little of this mystery every day. Never lose a holy curiosity." Curiosity drives our thirst to understand. It is the engine that drives good thinking. Sadly, we have been conditioned by negative responses to our curiosity. Things usually seem easier if we simply abandon our curiosities and stick to the status quo. The easy road, however, doesn't often lead us to the desired goal. Your ministry needs questions to be asked—especially the hard ones. If one person isn't clear on something, chances are others will be confused as well. When you've got a heart that seeks understanding, it's good to ask questions.

Like the little ones we teach, we need to maintain a "holy curiosity." We need to ask, Why?

The Next Step in Answering the "Why" Question

Not long ago, a children's pastor said to me, "Steve, we are really struggling in our ministry because so many of our team members, both our staff and volunteers, are all working off of different definitions of why we are here and what we are doing. It has created nothing but chaos." This children's ministry leader was describing the struggles and obstacles that were limiting his ministry's potential.

This is a classic example of why answering the "why" question is so necessary to maximize the effectiveness of your ministry. With that in mind, let's take a closer look at the first step: the importance of finding a mission statement for your ministry.

What's a mission statement? A mission statement is a brief but complete description of the overall purpose of your ministry to children. It's the next step in articulating the reason your ministry exists and what you do in a clear, concise sentence.

Asking Why in Children's Ministry

The first question we ask is the foundation for every other question from this point on: Why does our ministry exist? I know some children's leaders who can recite a long and complicated answer to the why question. It can sound super spiritual, but in a moment of honesty, many would probably admit they don't know the deeper reason their ministry exists. I know other children's leaders who would have no answer to the question. They are busy with tons of activities, but there is no balance, intentionality, or real health.

I know a little something about this type of leader, because I was that leader. Ministries like these can still be good and produce some fruit. But I know from experience that the fruit produced from this type of ministry is not what it could be. I wrongly assumed that my activity equaled effectiveness. There was always something going on, but each activity was an island of its own. There was no intentionality or connection between activities. It was random.

There are times where being random can be fun. But you cannot build a healthy ministry on randomness. It will leave you frustrated, tired, and wondering if anything you are doing is making a difference. So where do we begin? The answer for "why does my ministry exist" is made clear in the purposes God laid out for the church.

The Purposes Answer the Question "Why Do We Exist?"

Pastor Rick Warren has said many times, "You don't create the purposes, you discover them." The purposes are not a new concept or approach to ministry—they are clearly laid out for us in God's Word. These biblical purposes are worship, belong, grow, serve, and share. Ministry leaders who actually implement the purposes of God will reach their full ministry potential.

The following statement in *The Purpose Driven Church* captures one of the most profound aha moments I experienced throughout my initial quest in discovering how to reach my full ministry potential:

> Strong churches are built on purpose! By focusing equally on all five of the New Testament purposes of the church, your church will develop the healthy balance that makes lasting growth possible. Proverbs 19:21 says, 'Many are the plans in a person's heart, but it is the Lord's purpose that prevails.' Plans, programs, and personalities don't last. But God's purposes will last. Unless the driving force behind a church is biblical, the health and growth of the church will never be what God intended. Strong churches are not built on programs, personalities, or gimmicks. They are built on the eternal purposes of God.[5]

The five major purposes of the church are found in two passages of the New Testament that Christians all over the world call "great." They are the Great Commandment and the Great Commission. In *The Purpose Driven Church*, Pastor Rick Warren derives the five purposes of the church from these two key passages. We'll dig into these in more detail so we can have a purposeful ministry aligned with God's will.

The Great Commandment and the Great Commission give us the essential elements of a healthy, balanced, and biblical church based on the five purposes of God: Worship, Serve, Share, Belong, and Grow. In Matthew 22:37, Jesus said, "Love the Lord your God." That is where we get the word Worship. But Jesus also instructs us to "Love your neighbor" (v. 39). That is where

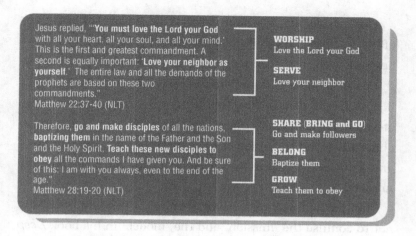

we get the word Serve. Next, we are commissioned to "Go and make followers." That is the word Share—and there are two important components to Share: Bring and Go. We want kids to Bring their friends to church and we want them to Go out into the community and share God's love. Then in Matthew 28:19, we're instructed to "baptize them." That is where we get the word Belong. And lastly, in verse 20, we're commanded to "teach them to obey." That is where we get the word Grow.

By aligning the purposes of the church in our children's ministry, we create balance. Here is an example of how we state these purposes in Saddleback Kids in the order of our discipleship process:

Jesus' Statement Is Our Purpose

Love the Lord your God—Worship

Baptize them—Belong

Teach them to obey—Grow

Love your neighbor—Serve

Go and make followers—Share (Bring and Go)

These five purposes summarize God's heart for every one of his disciples, and that includes children. For this reason, we begin with the five purposes of God as the foundation for everything we do in our children's ministry. While each ministry may have different ideas on how to fulfill the five purposes and operate with different styles, there should not be any disagreement about what God has called us to do in the Great Commandment and the Great Commission because God's purposes are the mission!

Let me add a quick word of warning. We should be careful not to confuse the "mission" and the "model." In his book *Deep and Wide*, Andy Stanley says it this way, "A church model is essentially the framework a church or denomination chooses or creates to advance its specific vision."[6] Models, programs, and styles are simply the means to an end, but they have a shelf life. At some point, the models that work today will no longer be effective. However, the mission never changes or loses impact. How can we know that? Because the mission is based on the purposes found in the unchanging word of God.

To further our understanding of the purposes, let's take a few moments to dive a little deeper into each of them.

Purpose 1: Worship—"Love the Lord your God with all your heart"

Our first purpose is to live a life of worship and devotion to God. Jesus recites the instructions to "Worship the Lord your God, and serve him only" in Matthew 4:10 during one of his most difficult trials. Scripture admonishes us to celebrate God's presence by magnifying the Lord and exalting him. Psalm 34:3 says, "O magnify the LORD with me, and let us exalt his name together" (KJV).

We want our children to understand that worship is more than just singing songs. There are two arenas of worship. First, the Scripture tells us that the way we live our lives is an act of worship to God. We present ourselves to God daily as a spiritual act of worship. That's why Paul says, "I plead with you to give your bodies to God because of all he has done for you. Let them be a living and holy sacrifice—the kind he will find acceptable. This is truly the way to worship him" (Rom. 12:1 NLT).

Second, we gather together each week as a church body to "magnify the Lord" and encourage one another together in corporate worship. Like Psalm 122:1 says, "I was glad when they said to me, 'Let us go to the house of the LORD'" (NLT).

Purpose 2: Belong—"Baptize them"

As Christians, we are called to belong and not just believe. We are not meant to do life alone. While baptism is an outward symbol of a person's decision to make Christ the Lord of their life, it is also a symbol of fellowship with other believers. It not only symbolizes our new life in Christ, but it also visualizes a person's incorporation into the body of Christ.

Children want to know they are welcome. They want to be known and to know others. Ephesians 2:19 says, "You are members of God's very own family, citizens of God's country, and you belong in God's household with every other Christian" (TLB). When children reach the stage of life when they can understand their need for salvation, are willing to make Christ the Lord of their life, and are able to articulate their understanding and belief, then we say they have reached the age of accountability and they are ready to join the body of Christ in an official way (even though they may have grown up in the church). That's why we at Saddleback baptize kids—to show they belong to Christ and they belong to a family of believers.

Purpose 3: Grow—"Teach them to obey"

The purpose word "grow" represents the process of helping people become more like Christ in their thoughts, feelings, and actions. We are called not only to reach people but also to teach them. It is God's desire for every believer to grow and mature in their spiritual journey. As Paul writes, "Build up the church, the body of Christ. This will continue until we all come to such unity in our faith and knowledge of God's Son that we will be mature in the Lord, measuring up to the full and complete standard of Christ" (Eph. 4:12–13 NLT; see also Col. 2:6–7). We are clearly instructed to help our children grow in their faith. As a child grows and develops in their relationship with Christ, their "roots" become increasingly deeper and more strongly connected to Christ—the One who gives everything necessary for true life!

Purpose 4: Serve—"Love your neighbor as yourself"

Serving "our neighbor" demonstrates God's love by meeting their needs and healing their hurts in the name of Jesus. A healthy children's ministry provides children an opportunity to meet the needs of others and exercise the gifts and talents that God invested in each one of them. "God has given each of you a gift from his great variety of spiritual gifts. Use them well to serve one another" (1 Peter 4:10 NLT; see also Eph. 4:12).

Your service to others may be greeting in the children's room, helping to set up or tear down, working the sound board, or helping to lead worship (just to name a few). There are so many things a child can do to "love their neighbor" by serving, and we as church leaders need to give them the opportunity. We must teach our kids to love others by serving them. This happens both inside and outside the walls of a church. Serving is a necessary component in a balanced ministry.

Purpose 5: Share (Bring and Go)—"Go make followers"

As believers, we have a clear mission to tell the world the good news of Christ. We have the opportunity to tell the world of his death, resurrection, and return that's coming soon. The commission to share Christ is more than a responsibility—it is our privilege! This commission to "share" (as we call it) includes two major parts:

> Bring—bring your friends to church
> Go—go and take the message of Christ outside the church

We first teach our kids to bring their friends to church on the weekends. We try to keep this purpose at the forefront of our mind as we prepare and plan our weekend experience. This is an opportunity for our children to share Christ personally.

We also teach our kids what it means to go and take the message of Christ to those who cannot or will not come to church. It is important for us to model and provide an opportunity for kids to share Christ through both local and global mission opportunities.

Altogether these five purposes from the Great Commandment and the Great Commission—Worship, Belong, Grow, Serve, and Share—provide us with the essential elements of a healthy, balanced, and biblically based children's ministry in the church. They serve as the foundation on which our intentional discipleship process is built. This process exists to move children toward spiritual health. So, beginning with the five purposes we've outlined, the key is to define your mission with language that makes sense to your church, your leaders, and your volunteers. That way you can align your team under a common mission and vision.

The Importance of Defining Our Ministry's Mission

By the end of this chapter, you'll have several tools you can use to craft a mission statement for your ministry. As you craft your mission statement, keep in mind the following reasons for making a written statement. Just as you need to provide reasons (your purpose) for your ministry, I want to provide the top reasons for defining your ministry's mission!

First, the most important reason to define your children ministry's mission is to promote unity. Why do we do this thing called ministry? It's all about introducing people to a relationship with God on this side of eternity—it's about what God wants to do in and through us! Ultimately, ministry boils down to living out the purposes and plan of God . . . not my plan, not your plan. God's plan. God's plan in ministry is unity. And unity in ministry is absolutely necessary. That's why Paul urged the church in Corinth to be united with such strong words: "I appeal to you, dear brothers and sisters, by the authority of our Lord Jesus Christ, to live in harmony with each other. Let there be no divisions in the church. Rather, be of one mind, united in thought and purpose" (1 Cor. 1:10 NLT). By defining your ministry's purpose, you promote unity.

When your ministry does not have a clear, defined purpose that everyone can understand and hold onto, the result is chaos and disunity. Having a clear purpose promotes unity and gives the team a rallying point, minimizing conflict, confusion, and frustration.

Another important reason to define your ministry's purpose is to provide a clear vision for your ministry. As the proverb says, "Where there is no vision, the people perish" (Prov. 29:18 KJV). God's purposes help us to see beyond where we are today. They give us a picture of what could be and what we should strive for. Too often in children's ministry, our vision is limited to the next service or event. Without a clear purpose, it is difficult to see beyond next Sunday.

Clear purpose becomes even more effective with a clear goal. It's like what Paul said, "So I run with purpose in every step. I am not just shadowboxing" (1 Cor. 9:26 NLT). There is nothing worse than wandering aimlessly with no destination. That's pointless! In the example Paul gives us in 1 Corinthians 9:26, it is like trying to fight a shadow. Paul is describing a "shadow boxer"—someone who is just throwing punches but not really aiming those punches at anything. They are just uselessly throwing punches without a clear purpose.

When we define our ministry's purpose, it points us in the right direction and makes it possible to set clear goals that move us toward the objective.

Defining your purpose keeps your ministry focused. There are many good things we can pursue in children's ministry. But to be effective, we must focus on the best things. A focused children's ministry will have far greater impact than an unfocused one. Like a laser beam, the more focused your ministry becomes, the more impact it will have on your community. Pastor Warren writes: "Focused light has tremendous power. Diffused light has no power at all. For instance, by focusing the power of the sun through a magnifying glass, you can set a leaf on fire. But you can't set a leaf on fire if the same sunlight is unfocused. When light is concentrated at an even higher level, like a laser beam, it can even cut through a block of steel."[7]

God's purposes provide us with the focal point we need to keep us on the most productive pathway. I love this reminder in James 1:7–8 as James writes about unfocused people who are constantly shifting in their desires: "Such people should not expect to receive anything from the Lord. Their loyalty is divided between God and the world, and they are unstable in everything they do" (NLT). Defining your ministry's purpose will not only show you where to invest your time, energy, and resources, it will also show you where not to invest your time, energy, and resources. It's like the perfect peace given by God to "those who keep their purpose firm" (Isa. 26:3 GNT). When we have a clear focus on our purpose, there is peace and God-given ability to press on toward the end goal. God's purposes give us a focal point for remaining on the most productive pathway.

A Clear Purpose Creates Meaningful and Effective Ministry

If you have been in ministry for any length of time, there have been at least a few moments when you wondered if it's all worth it. We've all wrestled with this question, but let me encourage you. God's purposes are the most significant and worthwhile endeavors on the planet! His purposes are eternal. Nothing else I do in this life will last beyond this world, but the work I do that is connected to his purposes will live on forever.

Whenever we do anything, we want to know that it matters.

We want to know that our investment, our time and energy are absolutely making a difference. When you define your ministry's purpose, it gives meaning to what you do. In 2 Corinthians 13:5 Paul says, "Examine yourselves to see whether you are in the faith; test yourselves." Evaluating your ministry can be a difficult task. And there are multiple methods and steps that can assist in a proper and accurate evaluation of your ministry. One of the greatest underlying reasons to align your ministry with the purposes of God is that it creates a way to measure progress and remain accountable to the structure of maintaining a balanced and healthy ministry.

To get a sense of this in your own setting, try to answer the following questions about your children's ministry:

- How many children attend on the weekend?
- How many children accepted Christ and were baptized last year?
- How many children are taking steps to grow spiritually?
- How many children are serving in ministry?
- How many children are sharing Christ personally, locally, and globally?

Were you able to answer these? The five purposes described above give us a framework to measure effectiveness and make sure we are hitting the mark. Even though we're asking how many, I want to remind you that numbers do not necessarily equal effectiveness. The objective isn't big numbers, it's health and progress. At the same time, we should have a consistent means of measuring growth and change, since anything that is healthy will grow and develop naturally according to its potential. Defining our ministry's purpose provides us with a starting point for addressing these questions. It also provides us with one of several measurement tools we can utilize as we evaluate our ministry's effectiveness.

What Makes an Effective Mission Statement?

Now that you know the major purpose and reasons for crafting a mission statement for children's ministry, it's time to get started and do it! Make sure that you consider these nuts and bolts as you write and formalize your mission statement. You can even use the following elements of an effective mission statement as a heading once you've written it out. Let these five elements guide you as you craft your own statement of mission:

Effective Mission Statements Are Biblical

As we said before, the purpose for your ministry—the very reason why you exist—should be founded on the only thing that will not change—the Word of God.

When we build our mission statement upon the Word of God, we are in essence setting the very foundation for our ministry. That's the purpose of the section above, where we looked at the Great Commission and the Great Commandment. God's Word is the rock that will stand when everything else shifts, changes, or crumbles. Build your ministry on that rock.

Of all of the components and elements that make up the structure of our children's ministry at Saddleback Church, the only thing I will not change is our mission statement. Why? Because it's based on the Great Commandment and Great Commission. Yes, we might tweak a word or two over time based on how language changes, but the essence will never change.

The methodology we are implementing in our ministry at the time of this writing will probably not look the same ten years from now. That's virtually guaranteed. Even our vision and values may change, along with our structure and eventually our style. There comes a time when things become outdated or irrelevant or both. However, the Great Commandment and the Great Commission will never be outdated. That's why I'm confident that our mission statement will not change. The five purposes of the church come from God's Word, so I am confident we can build on it, because the Word of God is timeless and solid, never changing.

Effective Mission Statements Are Specific

Nothing becomes dynamic until it becomes specific. We establish a mission statement not to have a cute saying, but to formalize the reason we exist and the activities we do. It's important to note here that the mission statement does not address how we will accomplish our mission. The how can change as methods and ideas change. The methods we use today to reach kids may not be relevant twenty years from now. How we lead kids toward spiritual health will change, but why we exist and what we do will not change. That's what you include in your mission statement.

A mission statement includes a commitment to certain activities and purposes you choose. For example, the five purpose words in our mission statement (Worship, Belong, Grow, Serve, Share) clearly define why we do what we do and precisely identify what we do. If the mission statement is comprised of lofty and ambiguous words and phrases and is not specific, your ministry team and parents will ignore it.

Effective Mission Statements Are Memorable

Because the mission statement truly is the foundation for your ministry, the mission statement you construct should be memorable! We're not aiming for a paragraph or run-on sentence. Develop a clear, concise, and memorable sentence that tells why you exist and what you do. It's that simple!

For example, the five purpose words in the mission statement of Saddleback's children's ministry provide what I call memory anchors. If you know the five purpose words, there is a good chance you will remember the mission statement.

As you're writing your mission statement, test its memorability in terms of length. The longer a statement, the harder it is to remember. And if we can't remember why we exist and what we do, then we haven't set up ourselves (or our volunteers) for a win. A good test for memorability is answering this question: Could your mission statement fit on a T-shirt or be printed on a sign? If yes, then your mission statement is memorable.

Effective Mission Statements Are Measurable

Have you ever set a New Year's resolution only to discover that by January 10 you're already struggling to keep that resolution? Sometimes our goals are ambiguous and that leaves us hanging. Perhaps your goals looked something like lose weight, read more, be healthier, listen to quality audio, and watch TV less.

Those are great resolutions, but without clear numbers, it's hard to measure progress. Making them specific is better. For example, you might say lose ten pounds, read twelve books on leadership, eat a vegetable every day to be healthier, listen to three new podcasts, or watch TV no more than one hour a day. These are specific and measurable. Set yourself up for success early by specifying exactly what you want to accomplish. But making it measurable is useless without action steps.

Effective Mission Statements Are Actionable

As we saw in our New Year's resolutions example, simply having a cool statement on a piece of paper doesn't mean we're accomplishing that goal. We may want to lose ten pounds, read twelve books on leadership, and watch less TV, but if we don't attach action to those goals, they simply remain as lifeless words on a piece of paper, lofty dreams never fulfilled.

Your ministry's mission statement is more than a cool slogan; it's the foundation for everything you do, the lifeblood for why your ministry exists. If there isn't action coming out of your ministry's mission statement, it won't fulfill its purpose in maximizing your ministry's effectiveness or help you reach your goal of leading kids toward spiritual health. Establish practical steps to reach specific aspects of your mission statement.

Developing a Mission Statement for Your Children's Ministry

Now that we've established why you need to define your ministry's purpose and the basic elements of a mission statement, it's time to make yours. I have given you an example of how Saddleback Church answers the why question with the five purposes of God and what makes an effective mission statement. It's time to roll up your sleeves and write your children's ministry mission statement. You've got the basic framework, so you and your team leaders prayerfully seek God about this and put your mission statement on paper.

Visit www.childrensministryonpurpose.com to download the free discussion guide with reflection questions and activities for Chapter 3. You will spend time considering the value and necessity of a mission statement and then work through the process of writing a Mission Statement that reflects your biblical approach to ministry.

position

Where Are You Now and Where Are You Going?

Give careful thought to the paths for your feet and be steadfast in all your ways.

PROVERBS 4:26

The prudent understand where they are going, but fools deceive themselves.

PROVERBS 14:8 NLT

Now that we've identified why our children's ministry exists and you've started to craft that purpose in your own language, it's time to move to the second empowering question in this discovery process: Where?

This question has two parts: Where are you now? and Where are you going? These two where questions will help you determine your position points. The position points of your ministry are crucial because one articulates the predetermined objective or destination, and the other one helps you to be aware of your starting point. You must know both position points if you want to maximize your effectiveness in moving kids toward spiritual health.

For example, imagine you are finally getting to go on your dream vacation. After many years of waiting, saving money, and dreaming, it's finally going to happen. I doubt that you would haphazardly wander around this vacation wonderland and merely hope you find the landmarks and sights you have imagined for so many years. No way. You get a map and plan each day's activities and travels so you can maximize your time and get the most out of this dream vacation. That planning requires two position points—where you want to go (point of destination) and where you are starting from (point of origin).

To maximize your effectiveness in moving kids toward spiritual health, it's imperative to know Where are we now? and Where are we going?

Let's take a closer look at these two questions.

Where Are You Now? Clearly Identifying Your Starting Point

The adventures I experienced as a young man taught me this vital lesson: You can't get to where you're going until you first know where you are.

When I was a young man, I joined an outdoor club that gave me the opportunity to learn, participate, and compete in camping, backpacking, wilderness survival, canoeing, and other outdoor skills.

In one of our competitions, boys were dropped off in the mountains with only a map and a compass. Each group of boys started their journey from a different point on the mountain. We were given from sun up to sun down to make it to a determined destination.

I knew how to use a map, so I was voted the leader of our group. I was actually quite comfortable with the compass and map. In a matter of minutes, I had charted our course. My group had other guys who had navigational skills, so I figured we had the trophy in the bag. I told my crew that I knew where we were going and that all they needed to do was hit the ground running and keep up. You know what? They did. We were doing double time. We tromped through water, hoisted ourselves over rocks, and covered the open fields like a pack of gazelles. We were killing it! However, when we reached our destination, much to my surprise, the leaders we were seeking at the destination point were not where they said they would be. My first thought was, "Wow, even the leaders got lost!"

We waited for a little while. Then we waited longer, and I started to become concerned. I looked at the map again. Did I miss something? I decided to set a new course, and our group was hiking again. I thought maybe the spot was hidden just over a ridge. To make a long story short, we got so lost that the leaders sent a search party to find us! And you know what? I didn't do anything wrong in charting our course to the destination. The calculations were correct. The big mistake: I failed to establish the correct "fix" on our starting position. It doesn't matter how good your equipment is or how accurate the map is. If you don't know your starting point on the map, you cannot effectively use the map and compass.

I learned that it's essential to accurately discern the starting point. Without it, you will have trouble finding your destination. A key component in planning your ministry goals is an accurate assessment of where you stand. That's right, I said accurate. Honesty is important, because sometimes we think we are doing better than we actually are. Sometimes we think we are doing a little worse. Answering the question Where we are now? can be difficult, but we must look deep into our procedures and methods to truly understand our starting point.

How We Do Things: Your Church's Culture Gives You the Starting Point

In *The Purpose Driven Church*, Rick Warren says this, "Every church is driven by something. There is a guiding force, a controlling assumption, and a directing conviction behind everything that happens. It may be unspoken. It may be unknown to many. Most likely it's never been officially voted on. But it is there, influencing every aspect of the church's life. What is the driving force behind your church?"[8]

Ultimately, this driving force is what we call "culture," and you need to spend some time recognizing and understanding the culture of your church environment. If you don't understand the current culture and history of your church, it will be difficult to properly assess the effectiveness of some programs and even more difficult to implement change in those areas that are clearly in need of change.

Have you ever looked at a program or process in your ministry and wondered how anyone ever came up with that? Of course! We've all had those moments. We must remember that processes, programs, and methodologies are not made to last forever. They are created to serve a purpose, but at some point, they need to be reworked—or even replaced. This doesn't mean those parts of your ministry didn't serve a wonderful purpose. But these things have a shelf life.

A story from my life may help to illustrate this point. My family and I had just made a transition to a new church in a brand-new state, and I was acclimating myself to all the programs, services, and events in my new environment. It all came to a head one day. I was in my office with several members of the children's ministry team. I was listening to them describe the church, the children's ministry, and several other items unfamiliar to me. We then left the office and walked around the children's ministry area as they described what typically happens on a Sunday morning, the style of service for each hour, and the rotation of the kids. The process they explained of rotating the kids from one area to another made absolutely no sense to me. In fact, it was so ridiculous that I said to them, "This is going to change sooner than later. It makes no sense." But as they explained the history of the church and the reason behind their process, I gained perspective. I could see why previous leadership chose to do it that way.

When you enter a new ministry environment, remember that the out-of-date and seemingly ineffective programs and processes we might question now were someone's brilliant idea not too long ago. The key is to respect the original idea for what it was without holding on to it as something that must last forever.

Respecting the past is the first step toward reinventing the future.

All ministries and church families have their own unwritten rules and traditions that inspire the way they function as a group. This is what we call your church's culture. It is a "driving force" in your ministry.

What Is Church Culture?

This is how I define church culture: the accepted practices, behaviors, and customs that constitute the way your church does life together.

The culture of your church includes the attitude and approach of the leaders who make decisions. Whether clearly defined or assumed, every team and every church has a culture that determines how the church functions.

In his book *Look Before You Lead*, Aubrey Malphurs defines culture this way: "A church's congregational culture is its unique expression of its shared values and beliefs."[9] Simply put, the culture of your church is "how we do things around here." If I came to your church tomorrow, and together we worked through your strategies and objectives for the upcoming ministry season, at some point you would tell me, "That sounds great, Steve, but it's not typically how we do things around here."

You know what? You would be right to be mindful of this. It is not enough to simply latch on to something and carelessly try to force it into the current day-to-day operations. As we work toward positive change in our ministries, we need to be mindful of the existing culture, because no matter how good an idea may be, if it won't work in the culture of your ministry, it won't work.

There is a popular quip in management circles that says, "Culture eats strategy for lunch." That doesn't mean culture is the enemy of strategy. It simply means you can develop a strong strategy, but if you don't have the enabling systems within your culture to support it, the strategy probably will fail.

Oftentimes we misunderstand culture or even underestimate its influence. One of the reasons church leaders have such difficulty initiating change in the local church is they fail to recognize the existing culture and the driving force that culture has on everything the church does. You can develop the greatest strategy the church has ever seen for reaching kids and young families, but if that strategy is contrary to the current culture, and the culture has not been addressed, the strategy will fail.

Robert Lewis and Wayne Cordeiro describe church culture in their book *Culture Shift*:

> Culture is the most important social reality in your church. Though invisible to the untrained eye, its power is undeniable. Culture gives color and flavor to everything your church is and does. Like a powerful current running through your church, it can move you inland or take you farther out to sea. It can prevent your church's potential from ever being realized, or—if used by the Holy Spirit—it can draw others in and reproduce healthy spiritual life all along the way.[10]

This can cause enormous amounts of frustration if not viewed from the proper perspective. In fact, this clash between a church leader's vision or strategy for reaching lost people and the church's culture has led to many conflicts and resignations. That's because a firmly rooted culture makes no room for a new vision or strategy. This may sound discouraging, but trust me, there is hope. I believe a church culture can change. But an intentional process must be followed. Understanding your church's culture is the first step in that process. Before you can influence the culture of your church, you must understand it and learn how to work within it.

Understanding Your Ministry's Culture Enables You to Work with Your Ministry's Culture

The main goal is to not fight your church's culture, but as much as you can, to work with it to accomplish the objective of effectively moving kids toward spiritual health. Now there are times when we need to do things that are countercultural. Jesus did that. He was countercultural when he preached throughout Matthew 5: "You have heard it said . . . but I say to you . . ."

Being countercultural in the church can be dangerous. You have to carefully navigate the nuances of those waters. Remember that the main goal is to work together with the team to accomplish the objective of leading kids toward spiritual health. Health comes with balance, and balance requires intentionality. A big part of being intentional is understanding the culture of your team so you can be productive from within it.

"Okay," you may be saying, "but my church leadership will never accept changes I propose." That's okay. Many (and by many I mean most) of us face the same hard truth: our church is disinclined to change. That's just people, and the church is made up of people. Keep in mind that great works are built over time.

It has been more than two thousand years since Jesus' ministry on earth, and God is still working to expand his kingdom. God has the power to make anything happen at any time, but even he takes his time. We must have a desire to make big waves with the patience to merely stir the still waters.

Establishing an Honest Assessment

As we have discussed, you can't get to where you are going until you first know where you are. The most difficult challenge in determining your current condition is being objective and honest with yourself and with others. Above all, your assessment of where you stand must be accurate. The key word here is "accurate." It can be difficult to be totally objective about ourselves; it's equally difficult to be objective about the condition of our ministries. We tend to think we are doing much better than we really are (or much worse). The challenge is to accurately assess the condition of our ministry so we can determine the appropriate next steps as we increase our ministry's effectiveness.

Here is a key verse that highlights the necessity of an honest evaluation of your ministry: "Know the state of your flocks, and put your heart into caring for your herds, for riches don't last forever, and the crown might not be passed to the next generation" (Prov. 27:23–24 NLT). It's not just important, it's vital that we know the condition of our flock to clearly understand what adjustments need to be made to be more effective in moving our kids toward spiritual health. It's like what Paul said to the church in Rome: "Because of the privilege and authority God has given me, I give each of you this warning: Don't think you are better than you really are. Be honest in your evaluation of yourselves, measuring yourselves by the faith that God has given us" (Romans 12:3 NLT).

I want to lay out the key barriers I've seen among children's ministry leaders as they try to make an honest assessment of their ministry. Most of us have a lawyer's voice inside us—you know the one that can justify anything. However, what works in the courtroom does not help you when making an assessment of your ministry. Here are a couple of things to consider as you begin the process.

Don't Personalize the Process

Years ago, when I was a children's pastor in Chicago, I hired one of my key volunteers, named Randy, to come on my full-time staff. Just a few months later, Randy had the audacity to question a program in the children's ministry that I had recently innovated before his coming on staff. From my perspective, this program was much improved and succeeding. But Randy had a different perspective. He said, "We have to do something about our Sunday morning programs. They aren't working; it's a waste of time." I said, "Wait, back up. What do you mean it's a waste of time?" You see, he didn't know all that was involved in revamping this program. He didn't understand all the time and energy I had invested in this. He didn't recognize the fact that I was quite happy with the program. I was thinking, Why did I hire this guy?

But you know what? He saw the results and was right: We did need to do something about our Sunday morning programs. Its day was over, but I could not see it because I had personalized the critique. I had made it about my feelings and my pride about the program, which clearly was no longer effective. I was blinded to the truth because of my personal investment, and I was unwilling to admit that there just might be a better way.

Take it from me: Do not attach your identity or your self-worth to the evaluation. It makes the truth hard to take. Do not make the evaluation about you because that event, that program, that ministry is not who you are. If a program is failing, it does not mean that you as a leader are failing. Do not align your success or your failure with any program. Programs succeed and programs fail; that is just the way it goes. Sometimes it works, and sometimes it doesn't. Please understand that just because an event doesn't work, that doesn't mean you are a failure.

Similarly, don't make it about you when certain areas of your ministry are succeeding. Just because an event or program does work does not mean you are the greatest leader in the world. This type of thinking can create pitfalls for us that are just as dangerous as associating our self-worth to a failing program or event. In fact, pride more than anything else will diminish your ability to properly assess your situation.

Don't Be Defensive

Defensiveness will also cloud your judgment. When you are defensive about something, your vision is narrowed. There are things that others see that you may not. I always tell our staff that the person with the best perspective is the newest member of the team. You know why? It's because they do not have the history and personal attachments to programs and processes that you have.

As new team members share their perspective and vantage point, simply listen. I never want to stifle feedback or fresh ideas—I want to fan into flame the ideas of my team as they're seeing and sharing experiences with me. Do I adopt every thought, idea, and observation someone brings my way? No. I choose to listen and validate their ideas without being defensive in the process.

Be Willing to Call into Question Everything

You have to be willing to call into question everything (yes, even the ideas you came up with). This doesn't mean that everything in your ministry will change, but you do need to ask if you are mentally willing to change something to better the ministry. If it's worth calling one thing into question, it's worth calling everything into question. And spoiler alert: It's always worth it!

Now that we've established the importance of knowing the starting point and honestly assessing where you are, it's time to determine your position.

When we started this chapter, I mentioned that the where question has two components: Where are you now? and Where are you going? We've established where you are. Now it's time to start defining where you're going.

Where Are You Going?

The following conversation from the story *Alice in Wonderland* between the Cat and Alice reminds us that if you don't have a clear destination in mind, your journey loses purpose:

> "Would you tell me, please, which way I ought to go from here?"
>
> "That depends a good deal on where you want to get to," said the Cat.
>
> "I don't much care where," said Alice.

"Then it doesn't matter which way you go," said the Cat.

"So long as I get somewhere," Alice added as an explanation.

"Oh, you're sure to do that," said the Cat, "if you only walk long enough."

Alice was going on a trip without knowing where she was going. The idea of going on a road trip with no predetermined destination may sound adventurous, fun, and exciting to some while absolutely horrifying to others. I think much of your perspective to traveling with or without a predetermined destination depends largely on what is at stake. For example, a random day trip close to my home involves no risk and little investment of time or money. Compare that to a ten-day international missions trip with thirty kids. What's the obvious difference? The stakes are higher.

Children's ministry is not a random walk in the park. There are eternal ramifications involved.

We must always remember that the landscape of eternity is at stake, and a casual, random approach to ministry is simply unacceptable.

Determining Your Destination

As we determined in chapter 2, the ultimate destination of children's ministry is to lead children toward spiritual health. No leader should leave up to chance the spiritual formation and health of the kids in the ministry. We have been given a responsibility and opportunity to influence the spiritual health of children at a time in their life when they are more teachable and pliable than at any other point in their life. This should not be a random approach, but rather an intentional process that guides our children along their spiritual journey as God prepares them to fulfill their individual and unique destiny, and they reach their full potential as disciples of Christ.

Determining our destination begins by intentionally defining what a spiritually healthy child looks like. This will give you an inspiring description of what you desire for every child in your ministry.

This brings me to a vital point that must be clearly understood. While we are using the definition of a spiritually healthy child as our destination, we must not be confused about the process of discipleship. Discipleship and spiritual health are a journey. Spiritual health is not merely a calculated arrival point indicated by checking certain boxes on a child's spiritual health report or fitting a child into a particular mold. The journey toward spiritual health is a transformational and progressive process.

As the apostle Paul said in Philippians 3:12, "Not that I have already obtained all this, or have already arrived at my goal, but I press on to take hold of that for which Christ Jesus took hold of me." We use the definition of a spiritually healthy child as a destination to purposefully clarify the direction and development of the opportunities our ministry provides children on their discipleship journey. This destination will direct your thinking and planning as well as fuel your creativity.

Without having a predetermined destination to serve as your objective, it will be extremely difficult, if not impossible, to evaluate your effectiveness. If you don't know where you are going, how will you know when you get there?

Imagine you hired a general contractor to build a home for

you and your family. You sit down with that contractor to discuss the layout and design of your new dream home. You ask to see the blueprints or drawings of the home, but to your amazement, the contractor says, "Oh, I don't need plans. I've done this a hundred times before . . . trust me." Would you be okay with that answer? Of course not. This is your dream home. You have worked hard, made sacrifices, and saved money for this home that you will raise your kids in. Anyone who has ever built anything knows you must have a plan that shows the end result and lays out the process for building that structure. This is called beginning with the end in mind. Knowing the desired end result is the best way to properly plan and develop discipleship opportunities, allocate resources, and measure progress.

How Do I Define a Spiritually Healthy Child?

To give you an example, this is how my church defines a spiritually healthy child: one who is living all five of God's purposes (worship, belong, grow, serve, share). This is not a perfect little angel. This is a child who is actively pursuing all five purposes as described in the Great Commandment and Great Commission according to the child's developmental level.

Using the five purposes found in the book of Matthew, we developed this: A spiritually healthy child knows Christ, belongs to a family of believers, is growing in his/her relationship with Christ, using their God-given talents, and sharing Christ love personally, locally, and globally. This definition is our destination, the objective of our ministry.

To end this chapter, I want to leave you with this question: If your children's ministry stays on its current path or trajectory, will it lead kids toward the destination of spiritual health? If not, what steps can you begin taking today to change the trajectory you're on?

Next up: It's time to tackle the who question. We've talked a lot about the why and the where, but who exactly are we talking about? Are you ready? Turn the page.

Visit www.childrensministryonpurpose.com to download the free discussion guide with reflection questions and activities for Chapter 4. These activities and questions will help you better understand the culture of your church and children's ministries so you will know how to work within that culture to move the kids of your church towards spiritual health. You will also begin to think through a series of empowering questions to help you determine your destination (spiritually healthy kids) and learn how to craft your own definition of a "spiritually healthy child."

CHAPTER 5

audience

Who Are You Trying to Reach?

Then Jesus said to the woman, "I was sent only to help God's lost sheep—the people of Israel."

MATTHEW 15:24 NLT

Now that we have identified why our ministry exists and established where we are and where we are going, it's time to address another key question: Who are we trying to reach?

For many years I answered that question, Who are you trying to reach? with "Whoever walks in the door." I may have even spiritualized it to myself, thinking, Jesus loves everyone, so we must reach everyone. Certainly Jesus does love everyone, and the church body should be no different. But the reality is that we cannot effectively reach everyone. Answering the who question doesn't tell us who we should or should not minister to in an absolute way; rather, it's an intentional step that enables us to more effectively minister to everyone in the end.

In this chapter, we will consider the example and pattern Jesus offered in his strategic approach to connect with different audiences as he changed the world. We too must be strategic in how we connect with different audiences if we want to do our part in changing the landscape of eternity.

To illustrate this truth, let me share a conversation I had with several children's leaders. We were sitting around a table after a children's conference. I was talking about the challenge of attracting new families to our churches. The conversation went to friends inviting friends to church services and activities. One individual, who we will refer to as Mark, made this comment: "Our children's ministry is the best it's ever been. I finally have really good teachers in all the rooms on the weekend and our midweek services are awesome, but our kids will not invite their friends. The only explanation I can see is the fact that their parents will not invite their friends."

Initially, it appeared to me that Mark was simply making excuses. I didn't want to jump to any conclusions, because I didn't know much about him or his church. So I asked a simple question that struck a nerve with him. "Mark, who are you trying to reach?" In a moment of honesty, I knew this question would create a whole new level of discussion, and that's why I asked it. Mark seemed puzzled and somewhat frustrated. He said, "Everyone, of course!" Not wanting Mark to feel like he needed to be on the defensive, I said, "Let me reframe the question: Who are you trying to reach on the weekends?"

Again, Mark said with a slight huff, "Everyone." I pushed it a little by saying, "Okay, I get it. What about your midweek service, who are you trying to reach on that night?" This time he was clearly frustrated and a little annoyed, "Everyone. Our church is committed to reaching everyone in our community, period."

I love the heart and desire in Mark's answers. The only problem is it's never going to happen. You might be thinking, "How can you say that when Jesus told us to share his love with the world?" Well, that's exactly what I want to explore in this chapter. I have listened to church leaders make comments like "Our church is going to reach the world," and while that can be an encouraging and inspiring challenge to make a difference in our world, as I said earlier, it's not a practical or probable goal—it's simply too broad and too general.

I have learned over the years that when you try to do "everything" for "everyone" at "every" service or program, you lose power and effectiveness because there is no focus. Think about how you have to distribute your time. Have you ever said, "I'm spread too thin. I'm giving everything a little of my time and attention but nothing is getting enough." Many, many times over the years I have felt that no one was getting the best of me because everything was getting a little of me. That's what happens when we don't focus our time and energy.

Having no target audience for ministry is like a world with only one band. Can you imagine that? Who gets to choose the type of music they play? What about different genres? This certainly would be frustrating. That's why we have many different types of music and many different types of bands to play that music. Each band is targeting a certain demographic. They are not trying to appeal to everyone, but to a certain audience.

Think about this in relation to your ministry. If we are not intentional with our audience, we will gravitate toward trying to do everything with everyone all the time, which can limit our impact.

An effective children's ministry makes the most of each opportunity by targeting a specific audience.

Of course any child and family is welcome at your church. I can't imagine anyone misunderstanding this point in such a way that they would actually stand outside the doors of their event and say, "I'm sorry, but looking at our demographic report of the area, you don't seem to be our target audience. You should leave." We would never want to isolate individuals and leave them feeling alone and unwelcome. Nor would Jesus. But as we will see, Jesus was very strategic in targeting his audience, and he gave us a model that is still relevant today.

To better understand this concept of targeting your audience, we'll consider three significant lessons from Jesus' ministry that will shape the framework for our next steps.

Allowing Your Heart to Break for Those Around You

The first lesson we see in Jesus' ministry is that he allowed his heart to break for those around him:

> *But as he came closer to Jerusalem and saw the city ahead, he began to weep.*

LUKE 19:41 NLT

This event happened when Jesus was traveling back to Jerusalem to fulfill prophesy concerning his death and resurrection. He came to a place where he could clearly see the landscape of Jerusalem as he "saw the city ahead." He was all too familiar with the daily routines, rituals, and activities of those living in Jerusalem. From this vantage point, he looked out over the city and the Scripture says, "He began to weep."

While he knew the battle that awaited him in that city and was mindful of the pain he would endure, it was not for that reason that he cried. He cried because he was completely aware of the fact that God's people had rejected God's plan of redemption for them. He looked at the landscape of Jerusalem and could see their struggle. He could see their pain. That realization broke the heart of Jesus, and he wept.

Something powerful happens in us when the struggles and obstacles our kids are navigating move from our eyes (looking) to our hearts (seeing).

While the terms *looking* and *seeing* can mean the same thing as they pertain to targeting our audience, it's important to recognize the subtle but distinct difference between them.

I was by myself one day at a popular mall. As is usually the case with me, I was walking fast and thinking about numerous things at once. I passed by a group of high school students and suddenly heard a comment that stopped me in my tracks— "Pastor Steve didn't even say hi." I turned around to see a group of high school students, all of whom I knew and most of whom volunteer faithfully in our children's ministry. I felt terrible that they thought I had ignored them. I apologized and greeted them as I usually did, talked for a few minutes, and then went on my way.

This story illustrates an important point. It's possible to look at something and not really see it. I looked at them enough to not run them over as I walked by, but not enough to see who they actually were.

I believe it's possible to look at the kids in our churches and communities without actually seeing what their world looks like and the realities they are facing.

To help us truly see those realities, picture a typical day in the life of the kids in your church and community as a landscape. A landscape refers to the visible features of a broad area of land. To properly navigate any landscape, it is important for you to first understand the terrain, the specific geographic features. You may have a map in your hand to guide you from point A to point B, but will you be crossing any rivers? Going over mountains? Plowing through snow?

Consider this question: What is the terrain of the landscape the kids in your community have to navigate?

Survey the "Landscape" of a Child's Life

If you were to chart out that landscape, what would it look like? Picture that you're looking at a map representing the lives of the

kids in your community. What types of terrain are represented on that map?

The objective is to help us visualize our audience from a different perspective. Not just look at them, but truly see them by recognizing and understanding their struggles and pain.

Carefully look at the landscape your kids must navigate every day. What happens in your heart and mind when you look at that landscape, when you see the obstacles your kids must face every day?

Take your time walking through the questions provided in the downloaded supplemental material available at www.childrensministryonpurpose.com to create a realistic picture of the landscape your children are navigating.

When I look at the struggles and difficulties my kids must navigate, it makes me M.A.D. I think it would be an appropriate response for all of us to be M.A.D.

I want you to be Moved.
I want you to be Aware.
I want you to be Determined.

To be *moved*, we must be motivated to do something about what we see on the landscape map our kids are journeying through. What does the visual of that landscape do in you? Let it fuel your passion!

I asked you this question in an earlier chapter as we examined why we exist in ministry: What moves you? Well, I'm moved when I can effectively help kids navigate the dangers and pitfalls of life to a place of health—a place where they are secure with their true identity, they are living out God's purposes, and they are fulfilling their unique destiny. What about you? What moves you? Listen to those emotions and let them fuel your passion and motivate you toward reaching your audience.

To be *aware*, we must accept the reality of what our kids are walking through and not hide from it, sweep it under a rug, or pretend it's not there. Sometimes I turn off the news because it's ugly or disturbing or feels like an interruption or, at times, it makes me feel guilty. We cannot treat the reality that the landscape map represents like we treat the evening news. The map you charted isn't a cute little exercise just to fill pages. This exercise should open your eyes and move you from looking to truly seeing.

To be *determined*, we must not allow the size and scope of the problems we see to overwhelm us. But stay the course. Don't give up and don't quit. Real kids in your church and community are traveling through the obstacles on your landscape map, and they need your help. Don't throw in the towel when things get tough. Instead, be determined to do something about what you see no matter what the cost.

I hope your heart is stirring right about now, because seeing this visual sure moves me to want to do something about it. And when I look at that landscape, I know something must be done. God has placed you and me exactly where we are so we can help our kids navigate this landscape full of deception and danger. We can't pick them up and carry them on our own backs (even though that's what we would like to do). But we can be determined to do what we can to lead them toward spiritual health so they will be fully prepared for these obstacles and the deception of the enemy.

Jesus Targeted His Audience to Be Effective, Not Exclusive

The second lesson we see in Jesus' life is that he targeted his audience to be effective, but not exclusive. During Jesus' ministry he focused his message on a specific target audience, which may come as a shock to some people. "Jesus sent out the twelve apostles with these instructions: 'Don't go to the Gentiles or the Samaritans, but only to the people of Israel—God's lost sheep'" (Matt. 10:5–6 NLT). Jesus literally told the twelve apostles not to share the good news with the Gentiles or the Samaritans! At first glance, this may be hard to understand. In fact, this verse puzzled me when I was younger. Jesus said, do not talk to them, do not share my love for them, do not share the love of the Father, go only to Israel. What is this all about?

When you think about this, some of you may be on the edge of your seats and some of you may have your theological boxing gloves on because we all know that Jesus loves everyone, and he gave his life for everyone. After all, John 3:17 says, "God sent his Son into the world not to judge the world, but to *save the world* through him" (NLT, emphasis mine).

The story above, however, illustrates that Jesus was thinking about the big picture. We can learn a critical lesson about targeting an audience here. Jesus was on the earth for only thirty-three years. In those three decades, he was doing ministry for only three years. Jesus had three years to model for his disciples how to win the world. That's not a lot of time. During those three years, Jesus was modeling how to strategically determine a target audience.

We see this same principle elsewhere in the life of Jesus. This time Jesus was leaving Galilee and heading north to the region of Tyre and Sidon.

A Gentile woman who lived there came to him, pleading, "Have mercy on me, O Lord, Son of David! For my daughter is possessed by a demon that torments her severely." But Jesus gave her no reply, not even a word. Then his disciples urged him to send her away. "Tell her to go away," they said. "She is bothering us with all her begging." Then Jesus said to the woman, "I was sent only to help God's lost sheep—the people of Israel." (Matt. 15:22–24 NLT)

Here is a Gentile woman who came to Jesus and asked him to save her daughter from a demon. And he refused to help her!

Now this is Jesus who could have just said, "Go home, the demon is gone." He had done that before. Why didn't he do that now? Was Jesus tired? Did he not like this woman? Was he contradicting the truth that God's message is for all people? Absolutely not. Jesus had a plan, and that plan included identifying who should hear what and when they should hear it. Jesus was strategically determining his target audience with the goal of eventually reaching the world.

What We Learn from Jesus' Example

From these two stories about how Jesus chose to focus on the lost sheep of Israel, we can learn several lessons. One is that you cannot do everything at once. Even Jesus intentionally focused on strategic target audiences in order to effectively reach his objectives. For this reason, we at Saddleback Church do not try to accomplish every purpose at every weekend service or program. Everything cannot be done at once. Jesus was not trying to reach everyone in a single mission.

Following Jesus' example can be tough. As church leaders, we have to be willing to make some "unpopular" decisions in the short term to be effective in the long term. That's why he said, "Don't go to the Gentiles or the Samaritans, but only to the people of Israel" (Matt. 10:5). While Jesus did come to save everyone, in this particular moment in Matthew 10:5, he was focused on calling the people of Israel to repentance. The mission was to eventually reach the Gentiles (and the rest of the world), but Jesus had a short amount of time to set the stage for the long-term plan of spreading the gospel around the world. This is key: The command in Matthew 10:5—"Don't go to the Gentiles or the Samaritans, but only to the people of Israel"—was given before the resurrection. The Great Commission—"Go and make disciples of all the nations"—came after the resurrection. The kingdom would be advanced, but it would happen in stages and steps, strategically by audience.

Why is it important to target your audience? Besides following Jesus' method of ministry, targeting your audience gives you a clearer picture of who you are trying to reach and defines the purpose you are trying to achieve. This makes it possible to successfully develop the most effective pathways and programs while also giving you the ability to communicate more clearly with your audience.

What the Bible does not state is when, where, and how we communicate the message. Imagine you are asked to speak to a group of people on the subject of forgiveness. That sounds easy enough, right? What do you think your first question is going to be? Yep, you guessed it—who is the audience? Let's say your questions and the information you gather look something like this:

- Is it kids or adults? Kids
- What ages? Seven-year-olds
- Are they church kids? Maybe
- Where are they from? Southern California
- What language do they speak? English

Any one of these questions could completely change how you approach that audience. If you are told, "We are not sure about any of those questions," you will feel lost because the audience is so broad. But by targeting the audience, you significantly increase your effectiveness as a speaker for a single event. Imagine how much knowing your audience would help an entire ministry! Again, this does not exclude others, it just focuses on a certain group so that you can accomplish your primary purpose with them. Then, out of that strength, you can reach others.

Targeting your audience allows you to focus your creative thoughts, gives you the opportunity to strategically plan, and allows you to properly prepare for ministry events. We can maximize our influence by following the model given to us by Jesus and targeting our audience. Targeting your audience ultimately helps you to develop effective pathways to move your kids toward spiritual health. Later in the book, we will talk specifically about those pathways.

The Importance of Knowing Those around Us

Have you ever tried to buy a gift for someone you didn't know very well? Yeah, it's not that easy. It's hard enough for me to buy gifts for the people I do know. It's no secret in my family that it took me quite a while to get this one right. Year after year I would buy my wife Christmas gifts or birthday gifts that she never wanted, considered, or even liked. She was very gracious and patient as she knew my intentions were good, but I was missing the mark.

I began to catch on when she would hand me an advertisement for a specific gift from a store, catalog, or magazine, with handwritten directions to the store or online site where I could purchase the item. Yes, I did get the hint. It wasn't as if I didn't know my wife, but the problem was I wasn't paying attention to clues in our conversations throughout the year. When it came time to purchase a gift, those clues weren't in the forefront of my mind, and I would scramble to find something she would enjoy. I didn't become a good gift giver until I learned to pay attention and be aware of the things that were driving her interest. While I may not always hit a home run in purchasing the best gift, being aware prepares me to make a better choice.

Let's carry that same thought on as we consider our children's ministry audience. How well do you know the kids you serve? You probably know their names, and maybe you know their families. But beyond the names, how well do you know them and their world?

It's important that we not assume we know our audience if we have not spent some time understanding their world. Because of our ever-changing culture and pace of life, it's necessary for us to be proactive in knowing and understanding the kids in our church and those we are trying to reach. I wanted to have a better understanding of the audience around me, so I started with the geography of my church.

Again, I found in Jesus a great model for understanding outreach in terms of geography. This is the third principle from the life of Christ, and it comes after Jesus' resurrection. He appeared to his disciples to confirm their calling to reach the world by identifying four geographic targets for them: "You will be my witnesses, telling people about me everywhere—in Jerusalem, throughout Judea, in Samaria, and to the ends of the earth" (Acts 1:8 NLT). As a response to this passage, I got a map of the area around my church and drew a circle around it representing a five-mile radius. The circle represented the geographic community that is within walking or driving distance to our church. I started learning everything I could about the neighborhoods around our church and the people who live there.

Identifying Your Audience by Their Level of Commitment

Now that we have become a little more aware of the potential audience around us, we move on to the next step: identifying your audience by identifying each child's level of spiritual commitment.

We illustrate this process through what we call the Circles of Commitment. It's important to note that identifying your audience through the Circles of Commitment is not equivalent to giving kids an identity. Identifying your audience is not labeling a child or isolating a child. Identifying your audience by spiritual commitment is simply a means to effectively and strategically connect with a child.

In the Circles of Commitment, you can see, moving from the outermost circle to the innermost circle, the following target audiences: Community, Crowd, Congregation, Committed, Core, and Commissioned.

The goal is to move kids from the outermost circle of no or

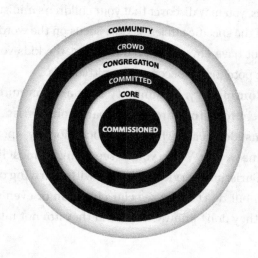

low commitment and low maturity to the innermost circle of high commitment and high maturity. Simply put, we're intentionally moving kids from "I don't care" to "I'm committed to share."

Working through the Circles of Commitment enables you and your leaders to identify those you are trying to reach. It also helps you to know what you are emphasizing so you can be intentional about balance. Think about how well it illustrates the process of moving the children in your ministry from the outside (low commitment) to the inside (high commitment). This is part of the strategy used to create the pathways that move children toward spiritual health, which we will cover in a later chapter.

Our objective is to move kids from the community to commissioned, from being uncommitted and unconnected to Christ to being fully surrendered to Jesus and sharing their faith personally—locally and globally. This rings true with our ultimate objective of moving kids toward spiritual health!

Let's take a closer look at each of these six Circles of Commitment and what exactly each circle means. As you read through the descriptions, you may discover that your children's ministry doesn't have one of the specific circles of kids. Focus on the word *potential*. You may not have any committed kids, but the kids you do have possess the potential to become committed kids.

The Community. Community Kids are committed to not attending church—they are living apart from Christ. These are kids who just don't care. They attend occasionally—perhaps two or three times a year. When you do see them, it's most likely at an Easter or Christmas service. They live within driving distance of the church but don't really see church as fun or even necessary. Typically, they don't know Christ, and they are not interested in church.

The Crowd. Crowd Kids are committed to attending our church—they are hearing about Christ. These are kids who regularly attend on weekends. You see them each Sunday, and they are usually pretty open and interested in spiritual matters. Sometimes the crowd kids are at church because their parents force them to come. But they're friendly and have even started making connections with other kids and leaders. They may even come to other church activities or programs, but predominantly, they're committed to their Sunday service. They have either made a commitment to follow Christ or they are interested in knowing more about Christ.

The Congregation. Congregation Kids are committed to a small group—they have a relationship with Christ and with other Christians. These are the kids who have taken one step beyond attending weekend services. They have definitely made a decision to follow Christ and they're committed to coming on Sunday. They're also committed to fellowshipping with those around them in a small group. They love being a part of the church and value the community and growth they are experiencing.

The Committed. Committed Kids are committed to spiritual habits—they are growing in Christ. These are the kids who are committed to attending on the weekend, faithful to a small group, and visibly growing in their walk with Christ. How can you tell? Their values are influencing the decisions they make.

The Core. Core Kids are committed to doing ministry—they are serving because of Christ. These are the kids who are attending on the weekend, committed to a small group, visibly growing in their walk with Christ, and are actively involved in a ministry as a volunteer. They understand that God has given them gifts and talents that are to be used for his glory, and they're sharing those gifts and talents by serving.

The Commissioned. Commissioned Kids are committed to sharing Christ personally—locally and globally. These are the kids who are committed to attending on the weekend, faithful to a small group, visibly growing in their walk with Christ, actively involved in a ministry as a volunteer, sharing Christ with those around them, and involved with a mission trip.

The Commissioned circle is our ultimate goal or objective. Will every kid hit this mark? No. If a child doesn't fall into the Commissioned, does that mean they're not spiritually healthy? No. Not at all! Can a child be spiritually healthy and not be a commissioned kid? Yes! Absolutely!

Our objective is to progressively move children through an intentional discipleship process that leads to spiritual health. This process is a tool to help us identify who we are reaching and determine how to keep the children strategically moving toward the destination of spiritual health.

In *Purpose Driven Youth Ministry*, Doug Fields describes it this way, "The clearer the picture you have of what each commitment level looks like, the easier it will be for you to relate to kids at their respective levels."[11] Remember, a purpose driven children's ministry is developmental. We are leading kids in a discipleship process toward spiritual health.

When the Importance of Audience Clicked for Me

Years ago, I learned a valuable lesson about the importance of targeting your audience. In America, Halloween is a prime opportunity to reach out to the community, and like many churches, the church I was working at hosted an event as an outreach to the community. We had fun games, tons of candy, and an epic family-friendly environment—the kids were having a blast! Because it was an evangelistic event, it was expected that we would share the gospel in some way at some point during the event. We planned that kids could come and have a good time with their friends, then sit and listen to the gospel, and then receive their candy. Simple enough, right?

But the turning point for me came in an exchange between parents I overheard. Standing in the back of the room, I saw one mom turn to another and angrily say, "I just knew it! I knew there was a catch to this Halloween event. I knew they were going to bait-and-switch us—lure us in to get candy and then bam! trick our kids into listening to a Bible story before they can even get their candy. Bait and switch." Ouch. She went on to explain that her kids had a long day at school, it was getting late, she had an early morning the next day for work, and it was too late now for her kids to even enjoy the candy they would receive. It was then that it dawned on me that I was hearing from our target audience—a family who didn't know Jesus as their Savior and felt we were tricking them into a scenario where they were forced to hear about Jesus. We had betrayed their trust. We hadn't properly planned the event with our target audience in mind.

Please don't misunderstand what I'm saying. The point of what I learned wasn't whether you should preach the gospel at your Halloween event. Each church is different. Every community is unique. What I learned was that I had failed to target my audience. Period. I had scheduled a Halloween event as a community outreach that ended up being planned for the church kid—not families in the community. When we target our audience, we can effectively plan to maximize our influence in ultimately helping lead kids toward spiritual health.

Now that we've identified who we're trying to reach and why targeting our audience is important, it's time to move on to the how question. How will you move kids toward spiritual health?

Visit www.childrensministryonpurpose.com to download the free discussion guide with reflection questions and activities for Chapter 5. These activities and questions will help you gain knowledge of the audience you are trying to reach, consider your community and church's cultures, and better understand the struggles and obstacles facing children today.

CHAPTER 6

How Will You Move Your Children toward Spiritual Health?

Jesus used many similar stories and illustrations to teach the people as much as they could understand. In fact, in his public ministry he never taught without using parables; but afterward, when he was alone with his disciples, he explained everything to them.

MARK 4:33–34 NLT

In chapter 3 we explored our mission and purpose and we developed a mission statement that serves as the foundation for all the other components of our children's ministry. While the mission statement establishes why your ministry exists and even states what you will do, it does not address how you will accomplish the mission. That brings us to strategy. Your strategy will answer the how question.

Let me start with a definition of strategy. Keep this in mind as you read this chapter:

> A strategy is a deliberate (or intentional) plan or method for achieving a predetermined objective.

Identifying your goal or objective is paramount, but there is another step you must take. You must develop a deliberate or intentional plan for achieving the goal or objective. That deliberate plan is your strategy. Simply put, your strategy is how you are going to get to your destination.

As we discussed in the last chapter, Jesus demonstrated an effective model for ministry in that he not only had a target audience but he also had a strategy to reach that audience. In fact, the strategy Jesus modeled was so effective that it is still being implemented today. Even more, the results are just as effective now as they were during his day. Jesus knew his objective, and he developed a strategy for how he would accomplish that objective. Mark 4:33–34 serves as a good example of how Jesus used strategy when he taught crowds: "Jesus used many similar stories and illustrations to teach the people as much as they could understand" (Mark 4:33 NLT).

Note that Jesus taught the crowd in a way "they could understand." The goal of his strategy was understanding, which is the path to authentic transformation. He adapted his message to the level of understanding of those in the crowd. The stories Jesus told the crowd revealed only a portion of the revelation in his message. But when he was with the disciples in a small group, Jesus disclosed the full meaning of his teaching: "In his public ministry he never taught without using parables; but afterward, when he was alone with his disciples, he explained everything to them" (Mark 4:34 NLT).

With regard to strategy, why did Jesus use parables at first and then explain them later on? Was he trying to confuse the crowds? Was he in a hurry? What about the crowds? Did he not care about them? Did Jesus not have a sense of urgency to "tell them like it is"?

I think we would all agree that the answer to each of these questions is a resounding no. Think about this: No one loved these people more than Jesus, and no one had a greater sense of urgency than Jesus. And still he gave them only bite-size portions of his teaching.

What was Jesus doing? He was modeling a strategy.

He knew his purpose and his audience, so he intentionally and strategically formatted a teaching strategy to connect with the people before him. Now the disciples were there listening right along with the crowd, but Jesus had a different approach and method for them. Once he was with his disciples in a small group, he revealed deeper truths to them. Jesus knew they were ready for it even if they didn't completely understand everything he said. The crowds were not at the same place in their spiritual journey as the disciples. And wisely, Jesus tailored his message to connect with the crowd at a level that would make his message digestible. Jesus was exposing them to the truth of his Word and his kingdom. He was strategically preparing the groundwork for the next step in their spiritual understanding and development.

Strategy Answers How You Will Move Your Children toward Spiritual Health

Jesus understood the importance of strategy. If strategy was important to him, we must consider how to apply strategy to our lives. His end goal, like ours, was to help people know God so that they would be transformed. Like Jesus with his disciples, when we're trying to move kids toward spiritual health, we need a strategic process. If we didn't have one, it would be somewhat like throwing the pieces of a jigsaw puzzle in the air and hoping they fall into place. It's possible that some pieces will fall into place enough to recognize portions of the puzzle, but I think it's safe to say it would be impossible for every piece to fall into place to give you a complete picture. With that in mind, I'm not saying the absence of a strategy means automatic failure for your ministry. But evidence shows that strategy increases effectiveness and maximizes opportunities.

In chapter 2, I used a story about LEGOs to make a distinction between random activity and intentionality. There is a time and place to be random, but not when it comes to the discipleship process in your children's ministry. It's like the proverb "Do your planning and prepare your fields before building your house" (Prov. 24:27 NLT). The writer of Proverbs uses this analogy of working in the fields to help us understand the importance of putting first things first. He urges us to not rush into "building the house" before we have given thought to the other factors connected to the end result. In other words, there is a process to any successful endeavor that requires thoughtful planning and preparation. Spiritual growth is a process, and that process is identified and clarified by developing a strategy.

It was not by chance that Jesus compared our spiritual development with the development process of a plant. Both the person and the plant grow and develop through a process. Jesus also said,

> The Kingdom of God is like a farmer who scatters seed on the ground. Night and day, while he's asleep or awake, the seed sprouts and grows, but he does not understand how it happens. The earth produces the crops on its own. First a leaf blade pushes through, then the heads of wheat are formed, and finally the grain ripens. And as soon as the grain is ready, the farmer comes and harvests it with a sickle, for the harvest time has come.
>
> MARK 4:26–29 NLT

The farmer utilized his knowledge and experience to prepare the soil and plant the seed, and then he let the ground do its job. The plant will not sprout in an instant and will not come out of the ground fully developed. It takes intentionality, time, and patience for the seed to grow into a fully developed plant.

The farmer doesn't know how this process happens, but that doesn't prevent him from going through the steps he does understand. He may not understand the science of what happens in the soil, but he has confidence in the process and has faith that his work will produce crops.

This is a beautiful example of the spiritual formation process and the strategy Jesus implemented to lead people, step by step, into deeper levels of understanding and commitment to his kingdom. The apostle Paul, following Jesus' model, said it this way: "I planted the seed in your hearts, and Apollos watered it, but it was God who made it grow" (1 Cor. 3:6 NLT).

A children's ministry leader said to me once, "We don't need a strategy. Man-made strategies just get in the way of what God wants to do in a person's life." While this leader had good intentions and truly wanted the best for the children in her ministry, her response indicated to me that she did not fully understand the importance of strategy. Strategy, when implemented correctly, will not limit God's work in a child's life. It will provide an environment for God to do the work that only he can do.

A purpose driven strategy is based on Scripture and follows Jesus' methodology. The process defines our part in God's work and we trust God to do what only he can do. So how do you develop a strategy that aligns with the example given to us by Jesus?

Defining the Components of a Discipleship Strategy

To develop the strategy that specifies how you will accomplish the objective of moving kids toward the destination of spiritual health, we first must define the factors that make up the strategy. I refer to it as MAP:

Mission + Audience = Pathway / Program

Your mission was developed by answering the "Why are you doing what you are doing" question (chapter 3). Your audience was identified by answering the "Who are you trying to reach" question (chapter 5). With those two components in place, you're now ready to design your pathways and programs to complete the strategy. So let's take an in-depth look at the final component of the MAP strategy: Pathways and Programs.

The Pathways and Programs

*Show me the right path, O LORD; point out the road for me to
follow.*

PSALM 25:4 NLT

When driving to the church office from my home, I do not
need to use GPS. I have made that drive so many times, I actually
believe I could do it in my sleep. In fact, I think a few times I did
make that drive in my sleep. But if I'm leaving my home on the
way to a destination I have never been to before, I need more than
the address of the destination. I need a route or pathway to get
there.

To move children along on their spiritual journey, we need to
develop pathways for them to follow with specific steps or programs on each pathway.

*Mark out a straight path for your feet; stay on the safe path.
Don't get sidetracked; keep your feet from following evil.*

PROVERBS 4:26–27 NLT

I offer this illustration to help define what I mean by "pathways and programs." Say you are traveling from Los Angeles to
New York City. There are several routes you can take to get to
your final destination. Once you choose the route, you follow
the directions and the route will lead you to New York. These
routes are like ministry "pathways." To help move you along on
your journey, there are stops along the route such as restau-
rants, gas stations, hotels, Starbucks, etc. These are like ministry
"programs."

The relationship between ministry pathways and programs works in a similar fashion to routes and stops. The pathways are the established ministry opportunities (routes) that your ministry provides for the spiritual development of your children. For example, the established ministry opportunities, or routes, our church provides children are events, weekend worship services, and midweek small group discipleship. The programs are the individual and specialized steps on the kids' discipleship journey that progressively move them between places (stops) toward the destination. Here is an example of how this works in ministry:

Pathway: Small group discipleship

Programs: Children's 101 Class (Belonging to Christ)

We'll dig into this example in more detail below. For now, it's important to understand that this aspect of the discipleship strategy development process is important because of one simple reality: Kids move along on their spiritual journey in a series of steps. Consider this illustration. If you were standing at one end of a room and need to get to the other end of the room, no one would expect you to do that in one gigantic leap. Rather, you would move from where you are standing to where you want to go in a series of steps. And more than likely there will be obstacles in the room you must navigate around to make it to the other side.

For this reason, the steps can't be random steps that just happen to fall into place. They are strategic steps designed to move you from where you are to where you want to go.

The same idea is true for our ministry to children. Our desire is to provide kids an opportunity to experience God personally and develop a dynamic relationship with him through a series of intentional and strategic steps. The most effective format I have discovered for this process is first to identify pathways and then develop programs for each pathway.

How Saddleback Develops Pathways and Programs

I'll use Saddleback's children's ministry as an example of how the pathways and programs strategically work together. Our children's ministry utilizes three pathways: Events, Weekend Services, and Small Group Discipleship. We'll discuss those in more detail later in the chapter.

To develop our strategy, we use the purpose words of our mission statement to identify the primary purpose. Remember, your services, events, and activities will meet several purposes at one time. But always having a primary purpose that focuses our efforts can increase effectiveness. Then we add the target audience to the equation. As with the purposes, you will typically have several audiences participating in a single program, but we have a target audience that determines how the program is designed and implemented. For example, our weekend services have the primary purpose of worship with the target audience being the crowd. The reality is we could have all six audiences attending the weekend services, and we may, on a small level, be indirectly accomplishing all five purposes at our weekend services. But we are not trying to do everything on the weekend. We have a primary purpose and a target audience that determines the programming.

Here is an example of Saddleback's children's ministry strategy using our purpose words plus our audience identification. These, combined with our pathway and programs, are designed to move kids incrementally toward the goal—spiritual health. (These are just some examples of the programs we offer.)

Primary Mission	Target Audience	Pathway	Program
Share (bring)	Community	Events	VBS
Worship	Crowd	Weekend Services	Large group worship service
Belong	Congregation	Discipleship	Class 101—Belonging to Jesus
Grow	Committed	Discipleship	Class 201—Growing in Jesus
Serve	Core	Discipleship	Class 301—Serving Jesus
Share (go)	Commissioned	Discipleship	Class 401—Sharing Jesus

The MAP—A Visual Representation of Your Strategy

As I have traveled across the globe and taught these children's ministry principles, I struggled to find one visual form of communication that everyone understands. Until I realized that there is one visual form of communication that everyone understands . . . the map.

This makes perfect sense when you consider the fact that maps are believed to be one of the oldest and most common forms of communication known to mankind. Maps are so common today that we don't think much about them. We have maps for everything you can imagine—weather maps, road maps, maps of the ocean floor, maps of the moon, social-economic maps, political maps, topographic maps, and military maps. The list goes on! No matter where in the world I travel, the one thing that everyone seems to understand or relate to is a map.

For this reason, we use the MAP as a tangible guide to help us develop, chart, evaluate, and even communicate the strategy we implement for leading kids toward spiritual health.

Mission + Audience = Pathway

The Pathways and Programs on a MAP

Let me show you an example of how the pathways and programs work together on the MAP.

To clearly develop, chart, evaluate, and communicate the programs of our children's ministry, we use the pathways that categorize our programs. Any program that currently exists or one that is being considered must "fit" on one of the pathways. Instead of making what looks like a city map, it seemed to make sense to use an island to represent a child's life stage in children's ministry and the different stages of the child's spiritual journey. Below is an example of the Mission MAP that shows the strategy of Saddleback's children's ministry.

Our MAP strategy reveals an X that represents the destination of spiritual health. There are a number of ports on the island that represent the pathway we call Events. We utilize Events to establish the initial connection with our Community and provide a pathway that moves them to the weekend service. Next, you notice a long pathway along the outer rim of the island that represents the pathway we call Weekend Services. As the MAP indicates, kids who attend only on the weekend are given the opportunity to progress toward the destination of spiritual health. However, the programs offered on the weekend pathway are not designed with the same level of spiritual depth as the inner pathway. Therefore, once kids begin their journey on the Weekend pathway, we encourage them to take the next step in their discipleship journey and progress to the more challenging and rewarding pathway that represents Small Group

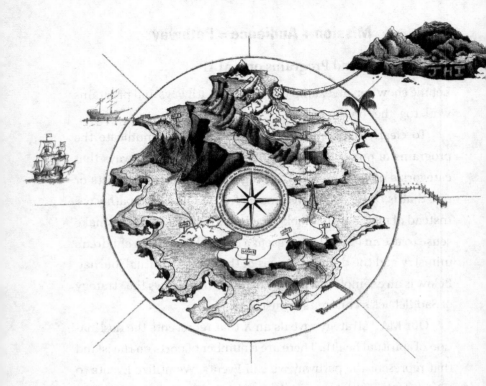

Discipleship. Each pathway is strategic and has multiple steps or programs. The basic idea is this: Get them on the island through the ports (Events), move them on to the first pathway (Weekend Services), and then on to the more challenging interior pathway (Small Group Discipleship).

Keep in mind that your pathways and programs will look different than ours. The point is not for you to necessarily adopt the pathways and programs of Saddleback Kids ministry, although that's totally acceptable if you do. The point is to show you the thought process behind each pathway, how each component of the strategy works together, and to guide your thinking as you consider the most effective pathways and programs for your strategy.

Here is a big picture overview of each pathway we utilize and an example of a program on that pathway:

EVENTS—Establish the initial connection

While some of our events are designed primarily for specific groups within our children's ministry, most of the energy we invest in event planning is designed primarily to reach and connect with the community child in our circles of commitment.

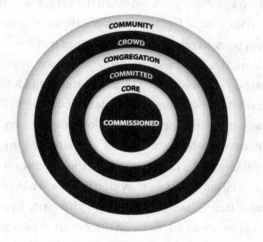

Target Audience: Community

Events establish an initial connection for those who are interested in the church but are perhaps unwilling, hesitant, or fearful to show up on a weekend.

Why do you think Jesus spent so much time at weddings, parties, and in people's homes? Simply because it was an opportunity to initiate a relationship and build a relational bridge.

Later, Matthew invited Jesus and his disciples to his home as dinner guests, along with many tax collectors and other disreputable sinners. But when the Pharisees saw this, they asked his disciples, "Why does your teacher eat with such scum?" When Jesus heard this, he said, "Healthy people don't need a doctor—sick people do."

MATTHEW 9:10–12 NLT

For many kids, an event may be their first interaction with your children's ministry, so we want to create a fun environment that makes them feel welcome, comfortable, and hopefully attract them back to check out the weekend services.

Events are the "easy ask" because they can be strategically designed to be nonthreatening to an unchurched child.

For an unchurched person, the idea of coming to church can be extremely intimidating and just downright scary. Someone who is not used to being a part of a church community can feel vulnerable or at risk stepping through church doors for the first time either because they don't know what to expect or perhaps have had a bad experience in the past. Events are an incredible opportunity to make an unchurched person feel more comfortable, at ease, and less threatened as they walk through the doors.

Here is an example of what a strategy might look like designed to reach the community:

Primary Mission + Target Audience = Pathway / Program

Share (bring) + Community = Events / VBS

Things to Keep in Mind as You Develop the Events Pathway

1. Strategically Plan the Next Steps for Those Attending Your Event

Random events can be fun and can serve a purpose. But most of the time stand-alone events take up our time, effort, and resources, and we are left feeling like it was a waste of time. I call events like that "appendix events." They exist but no one knows why and they don't seem to serve any purpose.

Our events become purposeful when we strategically build in a next step for those attending the event.

This next step may be a simple invitation to the next event which is already planned and on the calendar.

Plan out your events ahead of time so that you can promote "something" at each event. For example, if you're having an event at Halloween and you know many people from your community will be attending, then you can prepare to promote something really fun and cool that you're doing at the next weekend service.

2. Strategically Consider the Frequency of Your Events

"More" doesn't always mean "better." In fact, sometimes the opposite can be true. Sometimes in spinning our wheels, packing our calendar with event after event, we're actually doing more harm than good.

3. Strategically Calendar Your Events

When developing your events, you must always consider the church calendar and the community calendar. As much as you can, you want to avoid competing for the same audience on the same day with another group inside or outside your church.

4. Be Strategically Mindful of the Load

Have you ever heard the phrase "load-bearing wall"? It's a construction term used to describe the walls in your house that actually carry the weight of your house. These walls support the weight that is transferred down, called the "load," from the roof all the way to the foundation. These load-bearing walls have limitations and can support only certain amounts of pressure generated by the weight. If too much weight is placed on the load-bearing walls, they collapse

This metaphor represents a similar limitation when it comes to events. Events are different from the weekend service or small group discipleship pathway, but when children's ministry is responsible for an event, it's typically the same people implementing all the children's events.

As we plan and develop our events, we must keep in mind the energy and margin of the people who are implementing the event. If you put too much "load" on volunteers, they will either quit children's ministry or they will collapse. Either one is a sad commentary on our leadership.

Not only do we have to be mindful of the energy of the staff and volunteers, we must also be mindful of the stress and strain the events are placing on the budget.

Take time on the front end to really gauge your resources and energy. Is your team exhausted? Do you have the financial resources to do everything you would like to accomplish at this event?

Weekend Services—Expose Kids to Christ, His Word, and Other Believers

And every day, in the Temple and from house to house, they continued to teach and preach this message: "Jesus is the Messiah."

ACTS 5:42 NLT

Weekend services are the front door to your children's ministry. For some kids, the front door may be their first experience with your children's ministry. While the weekend service pathway has a target audience, it actually includes all children who interact with your children's ministry on a weekly basis.

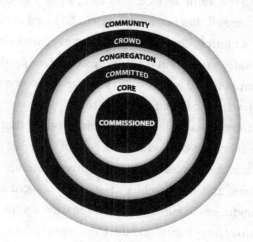

Target Audience: Crowd

They're coming regularly and engaging in your children's ministry on the weekend. They have been exposed to or introduced to Jesus, and they see the church as a fun place to be. Knowing this, we want to be the best steward of our time with the weekend service to fan the flame of the Crowd kids' natural excitement and commitment, ultimately moving and growing with them toward the next level on the Circles of Commitment.

Primary Mission + Target Audience = Pathway / Program

Worship + Crowd = Weekend Services / Age-level programs

Why "Weekend Services" for the Crowd Kid?

Earlier in this book I described my first experience in children's church. Stepping into an age-appropriate environment that was designed with me in mind was a game changer for how I viewed and interacted with the church. Growing up, I was used to attending the adult service, and well, while I love my Dad, it was never quite all that fun for me as a kid. I loved my experience in children's church because I could interact and engage with fun kid-friendly worship and teachings that captured my attention with puppets and leaders who knew me by name and built a relationship with me because they cared.

As we intentionally design weekend services that target the crowd, the teaching of God's word is central, with supporting elements such as energetic and interactive worship, fun games and activities, and media object lessons. The goal is to create safe and playful environments that resonate with the Crowd kid while meeting the spiritual and developmental needs of the other audiences attending the weekend service. Our prayer is that they will not only want to come back each week, but that they will want to bring their friends.

Weekend services look different for different churches, but there are several principles and big-picture frameworks we can all apply to the weekend services to connect with kids and increase our effectiveness in moving them toward spiritual health. Here are a few things to keep in mind as you plan your weekend services:

Get Their Attention

Whatever happens first in your weekend service should capture kids' attention. You can do this a number of different ways, like games and funny videos. But, there are other ways to grab a child's attention that aren't so obvious. For example, be intentional about making the kids who walk in your doors feel welcome. Let them know that they belong here. It seems so simple, but it is such a big deal. Another way to get their attention is to let them know you have been preparing for their arrival. How do we do that? By letting kids know they are wanted here! Focus on creating an environment that screams, "We did this for you" rather than "Since you're here..." This doesn't mean you must have a climbing wall, indoor petting zoo, go-kart track, and an arcade to create an effective environment for your large group worship. What it does mean is that you did the best you could with the facilities and resources at your disposal. Sometimes the simplest of things communicates a powerful message.

Get Them Interested

If a child is bored, they will mentally shut down. And if they're mentally shut down, you won't be able to effectively communicate and connect with them. The cure for boredom is FUN. Fun is the tool that opens the mind of a child.

Purposeful fun opens up the heart and mind of a child and gives us the valuable opening we need to communicate life transformation. Fun provides us with the opportunity to connect with that child on their level. It's possible to spend a whole lot of time and energy trying to get the child to rise to the adult level so that we can teach them. However, the more productive approach is to go to a kids' level and effectively connect with them in a relevant manner. This is the type of connection that allows you to teach the Word of God effectively.

Get Them Connected

If a child feels isolated, they will shut down. All of their mental and emotional energy will be focused solely on the fact that they are "alone and no one cares." Instantly, this will generate feelings such as "I hate this place," "They're not friendly," "I'm not welcome here," and "I don't want to be here." The cure for isolation is FRIENDS.

As you're thinking through and planning the flow of your children's ministry weekend service, ensure that every child meets one of the leaders in the room and has the opportunity to meet kids their own age. If we fail to get kids connected to other kids and to leaders, we will lose the opportunity to connect them to God because they probably will not come back.

Get Them Involved

Kids love interaction. As you develop your weekend service, strategically incorporate ways for kids to actively participate in the service. Be very intentional about including everyone and making sure no one is left out.

Get Them Back

Earlier I mentioned the Weekend Pathway as the front door to your children's ministry. If we are not strategic with this pathway, it can also become the back door. We don't want new kids checking out our ministry once and not coming back. At the same time, we don't want kids who call our church home to lose interest and stop coming.

To close the back door and keep it closed, we create an environment where kids arrive anticipating an incredible experience and where they leave with a sense of anticipation for next week. We want kids to love what they've experienced so much that they choose coming to church over other options that could fill their day. Another way to close the back door is to utilize an intentional follow-up strategy to connect with kids who missed for extended periods of time. It lets them know that you noticed they weren't there and you missed them.

Whether the kids attend frequently or infrequently, a clearly developed strategy will help you maximize whatever opportunities you have with each child.

Discipleship—Explore, Engage, Empower, and Express the Purposes of God

Discipleship is the pathway we utilize to move kids from the weekend services to the next level of spiritual commitment.

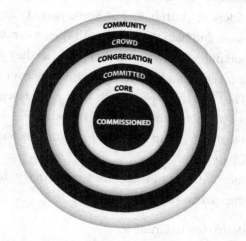

Target Audience: Congregation, Committed, Core, Commissioned

At Saddleback Church we call our discipleship pathway Kids Small Groups (KSG). This pathway is available for children pre-K through grade six and meets during midweek. It has four target audiences: the congregation, the committed, the core, and the commissioned. It has a lot of the same features as Sunday school except our program does not happen on Sunday.

Working through The Journey (our discipleship curriculum), the child will focus on developing a relationship with Jesus, learning what it means to be a part of the church family, and connecting with their peers and leaders. All of this is done in a consistent small group atmosphere with the same leaders, same kids, and same day and time each week. A typical KSG gathering will include Bible study and life application, crafts and games that relate to the lessons, worship through music and singing, prayer requests and group prayer, Scripture memorization, and serving opportunities.

Our small group discipleship pathway is strategically designed to involve parents in their child's spiritual development. Each week students go through their lessons with their small group and leaders at church, and at home parents are asked to review the lesson and help their kids with their memory verse. It is a great opportunity to grow with their child as they go through the questions together and watch their child discover vital spiritual truths. The time they spend with their child is a gift and an opportunity to impact their life on an eternal level!

How does small group discipleship work in Saddleback's children's ministry?

At Saddleback Church, there are two primary divisions on our discipleship pathway:

Pre-Kindergarten to Grade 2
Grades 3–6

Both of these divisions travel along the same pathway, but they have different programs. Let me take you briefly through each of them. Keeping spiritual health in mind, the main outcome for our pre-k to grade 2 is familiarity with the Bible and its teachings. The curriculum for these students focuses on introducing students to a relationship with God and what it means to be a part of the church. The kids learn about the major stories of the Old and New Testaments and the lessons God wants us to learn from those stories. We do this through the four programs that take them through the Old Testament and the New Testament:

- Pre-Kindergarten—"How to Know God"—Old Testament Part 1
- Kindergarten—"How to Obey God"—Old Testament Part 2
- Grade 1—"How to Love Jesus"—New Testament Part 1
- Grade 2—"How to Worship Jesus"—New Testament Part 2

The way we disciple during each of these programs is through a small group study of the Bible with Old and New Testament stories, life application lessons, crafts, and games each week. All of our activities in these programs are designed for kids who are ready to take the next steps in their discipleship journey. We have a time of group worship through singing and Scripture memorization, a time for prayer requests and group prayer, and an opportunity for parents to share in their child's spiritual growth at an early age through review of weekly lessons.

That's similar to what happens with students in grades 3–6. They have an opportunity to develop deep, consistent relationships with other students and leaders through four core programs:

- How to Know Jesus (What we call "Children's 101")
- How to Grow in Jesus (What we call "Children's 201")
- How to Serve Jesus (What we call "Children's 301")
- How to Share Jesus (What we call "Children's 401")

All of these programs are steps toward spiritual health. Let me give you an example of what small group discipleship looks like for upper elementary students in our strategy.

Congregation—Explore the Deeper Truths of Belonging to God's Family and the Purposes of God

Primary Mission + Target Audience = Program

Belong + Congregation = Children's 101

We call this program "How to belong to Jesus." In this program our kids learn about God the Father, his son Jesus, and the Holy Spirit. They also learn about sin, salvation, baptism, heaven, communion, and the five purposes found in the Great Commandment and the Great Commission—worship, belong, grow, serve, and share (bring and go).

Committed—Engage in Scripturally Based Spiritual Disciplines and Practices

Primary Mission + Target Audience = Program

Grow + Committed = Children's 201

In this program, called "How to Grow in Jesus," our kids learn what it means to be friends with Jesus and the scripturally based spiritual disciplines and practices we as Christ followers engage in to grow in our faith and relationship with Christ. Here are several examples of spiritual disciplines we teach in the children's ministry at Saddleback Church: Communion, Silence, Prayer, Fasting, Belonging to God's family, Giving/Tithing, Scripture Memorization.

Core—Empower the Unique Design and Purpose Given by God through Serving

Primary Mission + Target Audience = Program

Serve + Core = Children's 301

This program is called "How to Serve Jesus" and teaches kids about serving. Not only do they learn about serving but are also given the opportunity to put what they have learned into action by volunteering in ministry both inside and outside the church.

Commissioned—Express Love and Devotion to Christ by Sharing Our Faith

Primary Mission + Target Audience = Program

Share (go) + Commissioned = Children's 401

This program is called "How to Share Jesus." This step is designed to help kids discover and understand their mission to go out and share Christ personally, locally, and globally.

Developing Your Pathways and Programs

As you develop your pathways and programs, it's important to remember that there is no correct number of pathways or programs. Each church is different, and the pathways and programs will vary in style, number, and implementation. For example, I know a children's ministry leader who has two primary pathways—Events and Weekend Services. That means the programs or steps he and his team develop must fit on to one of two pathways. The goal is not to establish a certain number of pathways or programs, the goal is to discover what pathways are available for you to utilize and identify the best programs to progressively move your kids toward the destination of spiritual health.

To develop your children's ministry strategy, follow the same formula that we've used as a starting point:

$$\text{Mission} + \text{Audience} = \text{Pathway}$$

If you find that you have a new formula or a different way of framing your strategy, by all means, use it! Whatever you do, make sure to be intentional, thoughtful, and prayerful.

Reasons for Using a Ministry MAP

Now that I've laid out what a children's Ministry MAP looks like, I want to make the case for you to make your own. While it may sound like "just another thing to do," in the end it should eliminate many things that you don't want to do—like deal with a chaotic children's ministry! That's no fun for the leadership, volunteers, or the children. Let me share with you the importance and benefits of developing a Mission MAP to illustrate the strategy of your children's ministry.

First, the Mission MAP shows at a glance the big picture of a ministry. I know from experience that it's all too easy to get lost in the day-to-day busyness of children's ministry and lose sight of the big picture. Charting your strategy on a map keeps you aware of the objective and how you are reaching that objective. In a single glance, you can see the big picture and be reminded that you have committed yourself to something that is making a difference in the lives of the kids you serve.

Consider how effective a tool the Mission MAP is for communication. Maps transcend language and cultural barriers—everyone understands maps! The Mission MAP tells a story about your children's ministry. This creates clarity. The Mission MAP also helps you to clearly show parents where you are taking their kids. Plus, it's a great tool for showing potential volunteers that your ministry is strategic and purposeful.

Having a clear visual map of your ministry is powerful. Take for example a story from one of my team members. In 2014, I went with a team to a *Purpose Driven Children's Ministry* conference overseas in Manila in the Philippines. On the day of the conference, everything was in place. Pastor Steve was up and running, everything was on schedule, and things were going as planned. Minutes into the teaching, the man next to me started to fidget in his seat. I discretely asked if he was all right. He explained that he was hearing impaired and that he had just realized there would be no sign language assistance during the program. He said he could read lips, but because of the room setup, he was not able to see Pastor Steve well enough to catch what he was saying.

Now, here was this kind gentleman, a loving servant of the Lord, ready to soak up as much knowledge as he could, yet he was missing it. He politely asked me to repeat what Pastor Steve was saying, but with more volume and emphasis—and directly into his ear. What could I say except that I would do my best.

We were off to a rocky start as I struggled to keep up with information. Throw in a "repeat that please" here and there with some odd looks from other attendees in the room, and we had ourselves quite an awkward situation.

Then Pastor Steve brought out the Mission MAP. Thank the good Lord, the man was able to see it. That visual representation of each step in the purpose driven model allowed him to picture, in his mind, what he was trying to understand. He was elated and spent the rest of the day diligently making notes in his workbook.

That was such an eye-opening moment for me. I saw firsthand how effective this model can be at bridging the gap between confusion and productive ministry practices. And that gentleman left the conference filled with excitement and confidence and ready to launch his ministry. Even if your volunteers and ministry team are not deaf, they still might struggle to really hear your vision and your strategy. No matter how much you say it, some people just have to see it. Depending on a person's learning style, they may not truly "get it" until they see it. You want to give everyone the opportunity to "get it," because that will make your team unity stronger.

Another major benefit of the Mission MAP is that it shows relationship and connection between how different components of your children's ministry work together and relate to one another. This can get complicated (especially with a larger church), so it's important to show how everything works together toward a specific goal. The Mission MAP helps everyone to identify the programs that are synchronized and working together as well as the programs that stand in isolation and do not really function as a step that moves the children toward the destination. Evaluating the relationship and connection between pathways and programs is vital in understanding the effectiveness of each step we provide for our kids.

Then consider how the Mission MAP will help you balance your ministry. Unless you set up an intentional plan to balance the five purposes of the church—giving equal emphasis to worship, belong, grow, serve, share—you will tend to overemphasize what the leader is most passionate about. If you're the most passionate about worship, your children's ministry will strongly emphasize worship and perhaps not guide kids through the other four purposes. By charting our pathways and programs on the Mission MAP, you will be able to see and identify areas that may be out of balance and create the appropriate action plan to establish the balance you desire. I have discovered this level of accountability to be one of the keys for developing health in a children's ministry.

Implementing Your Strategy

Good planning and hard work lead to prosperity, but hasty shortcuts lead to poverty.

PROVERBS 21:5 NLT

Have you ever heard the expression "out of sight, out of mind"? That phrase is relevant for our topic, because sight is vital for memory. If we can help our people remember our mission, audience, and pathways, we'll be on our way to a healthier ministry. A story to illustrate: Years ago I did something very out of character for me—I did my Christmas shopping early. I found a good deal on a video game system in September and bought it as a present for my sons, so I hid the new game system in the garage in a place where only I could find it. The problem was Christmas was three months away, and a lot can happen in three months.

Christmas came and went. I never thought about that present. Fast-forward six months to June. I'm in the garage looking for something, and there, buried underneath mounds of stuff, was the brand-new video game system that I intended to give my sons for Christmas. The truth hit me hard: out of sight, out of mind.

The danger is this same "out of sight, out of mind" scenario can happen with our ministries. I remember many years ago when the senior pastor of the church I was serving gave each pastor on our staff a copy of the book *The Purpose Driven Church*. During our weekly pastors' meeting, we set aside time to discuss the book as a team. We had some great discussions as different aspects of the purpose driven methodology challenged our assumptions about the way we approached ministry in our church. There were several memorable moments from those discussions, but one I'll never forget.

We were discussing chapters 4 and 5 of the book, which outline the need to establish the purpose of your ministry and develop a mission statement. I remember one of the pastors saying, "We need a mission statement." Our senior pastor responded by saying, "We have one." This took many of us by surprise. Our senior pastor quoted the mission statement and said that it was developed years ago. The mission statement was well written. There was one copy in a filing cabinet. Very few knew we had one. Again, out of sight, out of mind.

Once you have developed your strategy, it must be known and visible, or you may find your ministry drifting off course. The strategy MAP is an effective way to keep the strategy visible and on the minds of those who implement the strategy. We should never assume the strategy is known or being implemented lest we fall into the "out of sight, out of mind" trap. Believe me, it can happen to anyone.

Moving Along

I hope that this chapter has shown you that knowing your strategy is very important, but it doesn't complete the job of sharing the strategy. My hope is that you've gained tools for creating a visual strategy and motivation for sharing it with your team in creative ways. It's like hearing God's Word—that's a big deal in itself, but it's not enough. We must put into action what we have heard. The same is true with strategies. The power and effectiveness of a clear strategy will not materialize without diligent action. Like it says in the book of James, "Don't just listen to God's word. You must do what it says. Otherwise, you are only fooling yourselves" (James 1:22 NLT). Now that you have answered the how question by developing your strategy with a MAP, it's time to move on to the fifth and final question: What?

Visit www.childrensministryonpurpose.com to download the free discussion guide with reflection questions and activities for Chapter 6. These activities and questions will help you identify the intentional pathways at your church, talk through a series of questions to ask your team as you create events, and work through another set of questions to ask about your weekend services. You'll also find a practical tool to use to create your own ministry map.

CHAPTER 7

structure

What Are the Essential Components Needed to Support the Strategy?

The human body has many parts, but the many parts make up one whole body. So it is with the body of Christ.

1 CORINTHIANS 12:12 NLT

Our journey together through this book is an endeavor to increase the effectiveness and health of our children's ministries and to reach our full potential in leading kids toward spiritual health. Let's pause for a moment and take a look at the key questions we have addressed so far:

We asked WHY does our ministry exist to establish our purpose.

We asked WHERE are we now, and WHERE are we going to determine our destination.

We asked WHO are we trying to reach to determine our target audience.

And in the last chapter we asked HOW are we going to move children toward spiritual health to determine our strategy.

That brings us to the fifth and final key question—WHAT essential components are necessary to support the strategy? Structure answers the what question, identifying and determining what needs to be in place to support the strategy. Structure may not be a popular topic with many children's ministry leaders because we're usually spontaneous, free-spirited people—but it should be. The structure of your ministry will enable and empower your children's ministry to successfully reach ministry objectives and fulfill its purpose. Ultimately this moves kids toward spiritual health, which is the one and only purpose of a structure—to support the strategy. And in supporting the strategy, structure sets up a ministry to maximize the full potential of moving kids toward the goal of spiritual health.

Structure and strategy work together to maintain balance in ministry. Remember, for your ministry to be healthy, it needs to be balanced. Balance happens with intentionality, and structure and strategy are a vital part of that intentionality. What structural components are necessary to support your ministry's strategy and to enable a successful journey to the destination?

Let me offer this definition for ministry structure: The structure of your ministry is the system of interrelated parts that work together to support the strategy.

What Type of Boat Are You Building?

The structure of your ministry is the backbone that supports each and every part of your ministry. Naval architecture and ship design give us a great picture of how a well-developed structure is necessary in life and in ministry. The structural keel of a ship is a beam that runs from the front of the ship to the back. This beam is the centerpiece (or backbone) for the hull of the ship. The keel determines the capability and capacity of the entire ship. As the structural keel goes, so goes the rest of the ship. This makes the structural keel the most important part of a ship.

The same can be said of ministry structure. As the structure goes, so goes the rest of the ministry. Just as the structural keel provides strength, stability, and support, the same principle is true of your ministry to children. So let me ask you, what structure are you building your ministry on?

An Ark or a Basket?

We all know the story of Noah and the ark in Genesis 6. God gave Noah specific instructions for the construction of a ship that would be capable of holding unprecedented weight and cargo. Think about it: Noah and his family were tasked with building a seaworthy ship that was 450 feet long, 75 feet wide, and as tall as a four-story building. That's approximately the length of one and a half football fields. Wow! Without a doubt, this was a massive boat designed to hold massive weight. That's a structure designed for a large capacity.

Now let's look at a small structure, built to hold only a baby. This one is found in the story of Moses in Exodus 2. In a desperate attempt to save her baby's life, a mother builds a small basket out of reeds and sends her baby, Moses, down the Nile River, hoping a good family will take her son in as their own.

Both the ark and the basket accomplish the same objective—to float on water. In fact, both the ark and the basket are considered to be a boat by definition. The same Hebrew word is used for ark in Genesis and basket in Exodus. While both were considered to be boats, they were very different in terms of reach and potential.

The structure of the two "boats" was different because the purpose and strategy was different for each one. Regardless of the cargo, weight, or conditions of the environment, both the ark and the basket needed a structure that would provide the necessary support, strength, and stabilization to accomplish their respective missions. You can develop a great strategy, but your strategy will not succeed unless the structure is built to support it.

Remember, it's not about the size of your ministry, it's about the health of your ministry. Structure is a necessary component to health. While the strategy is developed first, the structure is developed for only one purpose—to support the strategy. If your strategy changes, you must change the structure as well. One cannot change without affecting the other. Identifying and establishing a structure that supports your children's ministry's strategy sets you up for success in the long run.

Why is the structure of your ministry so important? Let me offer three key reasons for giving considerable thought to your children's ministry structure.

First, structure determines the capacity or reach of your ministry. Capacity is the maximum number that something can contain or hold. Noah's Ark, for example, had the capacity to hold one animal or 70,000 animals. The basket of Moses, in contrast, had the capacity to hold one infant. I'm not suggesting that a children's ministry is effective only if it has large numbers. But we must remember that anything that is healthy will grow and develop naturally according to its potential. For that reason, we don't want to dismiss numbers. The structure of your ministry will establish the capacity to which your ministry will grow.

Second, structure enables capability or potential. Capability is the extent of a person's or team's ability. Your ministry structure will either enable your ministry's potential or it will limit it. The structure of Noah's Ark enabled it to navigate the high seas and withstand terrible storms. The basket was designed to merely stay afloat for a short period of time in calm waters. The structure of these two boats determined their individual capability. Structure increases performance and maximizes everyone's time and contribution by minimizing the waste of time, effort, and resources.

Structure speeds up and increases productivity by creating clear lanes. These lanes identify and assign the various roles and responsibilities within your ministry strategy, showing how your ministry is organized and how each group relates to the others. With this in place, the team members know what is acceptable and expected as they serve in your ministry. The lanes created by the structure also increase productivity by clarifying many of the week-to-week action steps in your ministry and preventing volunteers and staff from wasting time getting unnecessary approvals or stepping on each other as they serve.

For example, when team members and volunteers do not understand the mission, vision, and values of a team, they often revert to their own style and preferences for ministry. This is not to say that the team structure creates robots that no longer need to think for themselves. Quite the opposite is true. The structure, by directing team members in the same direction, allows each team member to flourish in their individual strengths and talents without running over each other.

Imagine that you have 20 volunteers. If there is no team structure in place, each of your 20 volunteers may do ministry their way. That's fine, as long as it doesn't create conflict with the big-picture objectives or another volunteer. It's a major risk. If 20 volunteers are given the freedom to do whatever they want, however they want, you can count on conflict bubbling up at some point. And if there is no team structure in place, you have to deal with the same issue—20 times. Now imagine you have 40 volunteers or 80 volunteers. Without a team structure, you will exhaust yourself just trying to resolve conflicts and general misunderstandings that could easily have been addressed within your structure.

Not only will you burn yourself out, a system like this will frustrate volunteers and increase the likelihood of them leaving your ministry. When people volunteer their time, they want to know their effort and energy are actually contributing to something positive. A volunteer who feels their investment is a waste of time will eventually lose motivation and quit. Not only that, but they will tell others about their experience, which could create a negative perception of your ministry and make recruiting difficult. Bottom line, no one wants to jump on board a sinking ship.

The third reason structure is important is that it establishes clarity. I have heard some leaders express concern that structure creates limitations and restricts the freedom of flexibility. While the term structure certainly has a connotation of rigidity, it can actually expand creativity and flexibility by establishing clarity.

To illustrate, let's look again at the art and science of architecture. Did you know that a big city skyscraper is actually designed to sway back and forth with the wind and move a little bit on its foundation in order to withstand earthquakes? That's nothing short of amazing to me. The structure of the skyscraper allows for flexibility to avoid damage in high winds and earthquakes.

Your ministry structure creates flexibility by establishing clarity in areas such as communication, spending, priority in use of facility, and decision making. Without clarity, it's natural for staff and volunteers to make assumptions about the implementation of the strategy and their involvement.

Let's be honest. Rarely do any of us have absolute clarity in our churches. However, even though as ministry leaders we are not always given the luxury of clarity from those we report to, a well-developed structure will contribute to and maximize whatever level of clarity is possible in your ministry. I have found that a well-developed structure creates clarity by simplifying each aspect of your strategy. This clarity is necessary to keep staff and volunteers moving in the same direction toward the mission.

Developing the Structure to Support Your Ministry's Strategy

Now that you've got the reasons for developing structure to support your strategy, let's get started developing your structure. I will give some examples from my ministry, but the goal is for you to develop your own structure. There are structural components common to any children's ministry, and they're worth serious consideration as you develop your ministry structure.

While these components are common, that doesn't mean every children's ministry will address and implement them in the same way. Your ministry is unique and has a unique strategy.

As you write out those necessary components to your structure, don't stress about getting it perfect the first time. It's a process. Also, because your church and children's ministry is a living organism, there will always be a need for adjustment to accommodate growth and seasons of life. Take a look at your newly developed Mission MAP and ask yourself, What do we need to have in place to make this strategy happen?

As we dive into essential elements of structure, the purpose is to show you how we have answered the what question in our specific ministry and present some ideas that you might consider as you are thinking about your structure. Remember, structure will look different in your church, and that's okay. Your structure should be unique to your children's ministry strategy.

Even though our churches are all different, there are components to the structure of a children's ministry that are similar. My goal in sharing my ministry's structural components is to help you see how each component works together to support the strategy, not to offer suggestions for your structure. You might discover a component that is not a part of your structure or one that you hadn't given much thought to. If that's the case, I strongly encourage you to consider how that missing component might offer a necessary element of support to your strategy.

The Components of Our Structure

Saddleback's children's ministry has six major structural components. Most are typical of a children's ministry. A "component" is defined as a distinct part that contributes to the whole.

A structural component for your ministry is a distinct

The Components of Structure

VOLUNTEERS	The people who implement the strategy.
FACILITY	The place used to host your pathways and programs.
POLICIES, PROCESSES, and PROCEDURES	The rules and directives, specific methods, and step-by-step instructions that guide the operation of the team and implementation of the strategy.
COMMUNICATION	The means and the message you broadcast about your ministry.
BUDGET	The financial resources available to you for implementing the strategy.
TEAM VALUES	The core beliefs that drive your ministry and shape your ministry's identity.
VISION STATEMENT	Connecting kids to God and others.

element that has a necessary function in the operation and support of your strategy. You may include something we have not.

Volunteers. Obviously you can't implement your strategy alone. It requires a team. The volunteers who serve with you are so important to your children's ministry that an entire chapter is dedicated to that topic.

Facilities. This might seem a little obvious and possibly unnecessary until you find yourself standing outside a locked building with sixty-five eleven-year-olds expecting to have an overnight party. And by the time you figure out that you can't get into the building, you realize the parents who dropped off the kids have sped away. Another scenario is that you walk into one of the children's ministry rooms on a Wednesday night just before your midweek service only to discover that some of your supplies are missing. Then a volunteer calls to you in the hallway and passionately informs you that the tables and chairs are missing from their classroom, and how are they supposed to do a Bible study with no tables and chairs. Or you have a burning passion to start a new discipleship program. You have the resources, plenty of volunteers who share your passion, and kids who are excited to take the next step in their discipleship journey, but no place to meet.

I mentioned ministry environment briefly in chapter 6 as it relates to what the environment communicates to the child. And although it sounds like common sense, we must be mindful of the size, availability, and accommodations of the facilities we need to implement our strategy. You may have a great vision, strategy, and team, but without a place to host the program, it will remain just an idea. Once you have the facility to support the strategy, do your best to make it a positive representation of your ministry. Make your facilities the best you can with what you have to work with. It doesn't have to be perfect.

Policies, Processes, and Procedures. These three terms have similarities, but they're very different. They function together like the gears of a clock. Each one affects the others. I have never known a children's ministry to not have policies, processes, and procedures. I have seen children's ministries that needed additional policies, and some that needed clearer processes, and still others that needed better communication and documentation of their procedures. Whether these three entities are well defined, developed, and documented or not doesn't change the fact that they exist. The question is, do you have the necessary policies, processes, and procedures to support your strategy?

Use my definitions as you develop your ministry structure:

- Policies: Rules and directives established to guide the operation and implementation of the strategy.
- Processes: A particular method of doing something that involves a number of steps.
- Procedures: Step-by-step instructions of how the policies and processes will be carried out. These steps are a series of actions that lead to the same result each time they are followed.

Communication. Seems easy enough: You send a message, a person receives, done. If only communication were that easy. For some reason, the church world seems to struggle with effective communication. We stand on a stage and rapid-fire information at people, and when they miss the deadline for registration or don't show up for the event on time we say, "Well, it was announced on Sunday morning." At times we act as if the

Sunday morning "announcement" absolves us of responsibility when communication breaks down. The bottom line is this: As the leader of my ministry, the responsibility for clear communication rests squarely on my shoulders. We're talking about the communication that is necessary to support your strategy.

Communication is the means through which you promote your ministry and inform those connected to your ministry—community, parents, volunteers, church leadership, and the kids. Developing a communication plan for each one of these groups feels overwhelming to me, so I like to think of communication in terms of communication channels. A communication channel is a path for relaying your message and information. Think of it like a pipeline. You develop specific pipelines to deliver your message to a specific group. For example, with parents and kids, we use posters, flyers, videos, social media (and everything in between) to communicate and promote our ministry.

Another aspect of communication is an organizational chart. As we discussed in chapter 6, the Mission MAP is a great visual for communicating to your senior pastor, parents, and volunteers. When people can see your plan and strategy for moving kids toward spiritual health, it communicates purpose and creates a deeper level of excitement that words alone will not produce. In the same way, an organizational chart shows how the team is structured with its personnel. This chart visually shows who is responsible for what and how those individuals relate, communicate, and function together. Once you have an "org chart" for your ministry, you can use it to chart how many volunteers are serving in each area. This feature has been very helpful for me over the years as it gives me a quick review of areas that need more volunteers.

This story demonstrates the necessity of effective communication in your ministry structure. A senior pastor called me hoping to find some solutions to their desperate need for more volunteers. He said these words, "I just don't know what we need to do to get more volunteers for our children's ministry."

I challenged him to reframe the question. Instead of asking, "What do we need to do to get more volunteers?" ask, "Why aren't people lining up to serve in our children's ministry?" By simply reframing the question, he redirected his thoughts to structure. After a moment of silence, he said, "Honestly, I don't blame them for not signing up. We don't communicate clearly with our volunteers. They probably don't know who to contact if they want to volunteer. We don't have the most organized children's ministry in the world." He answered his own question. Much of the problem had to do with clear communication within his structure.

Budget. To put your strategy in motion, you need a clear understanding of the financial resources your church is investing in children's ministry and a budget that properly allocates that investment. A strategy without a budget is like a bird with no wings—it wants to fly but can't get off the ground.

A children's ministry leader brilliantly followed the strategy development process I shared in the previous chapter, but failed to address a key element—budget. She created an outstanding program, introduced the program to the volunteers, and created lots of excitement with the kids. But when it came time to buy things, she realized the initial expenditures and the cost to maintain the program was much more than she had expected. She had already consumed much of her budget with several big events. Church leadership said no additional funds were available. Had she considered the budget, she might have been able to adapt both the strategy and future expenditures to permit the program to launch. Instead, she spent a lot of time and energy on a program that never became a reality.

There is a cost to do ministry. You need money to support your strategy. But that doesn't mean you must have a big budget to implement a strategy that moves kids toward spiritual health. Since most of us do not work with unlimited resources, we need to be good stewards with the financial resources that God and the church have entrusted to us and establish a realistic budget for the strategy.

Team Values. Walt Disney, the visionary and cultural icon responsible for The Walt Disney Company, is credited with saying, "When values are clear, decisions are easy." In ministry, we often must make quick decisions without having all the information we would like to have. That's one of the benefits of values. Values make decisions for you. For example, when a question arises regarding the safety of a child, we don't need to call a meeting or even pray. We simply allow our values to drive our response. We've already worked this out before the Lord.

Team values are the shared core beliefs that shape your ministry's identity and determine the priorities and acceptable practices for decision making. Team values drive your ministry. They shape your ministry's identity.

I want to point out three parts to this definition:

Values are Shared Core Beliefs. Core beliefs are those essential truths that a team has accepted and practices consistently. These core beliefs are not casual assumptions or cute quotes that look good on a poster. They are essential truths that drive the action and create the culture of a team. They are "shared," meaning the team knows and implements the values.

Values Shape Your Ministry's Identity. Values set the tone, pace, and culture for your team. Values are the framework by which the team operates; they define how the team chooses to act and react. Values hold the team accountable and provide a layer of consistency so that the team knows what to expect. Values shape your ministry's identity.

Values Determine the Priorities and Acceptable Practices for Decision Making. The core beliefs of a team are actualized or activated in the course and direction of daily decision making. If the values are not connected to decision making and establishing priorities, then they are not shared core beliefs and therefore not a value. It's not enough to just "say" you have stated values. The values must be acted on or they are not real values.

When values are actionable, driving the priorities and considered acceptable practices for decisions, those values will influence the process in which decisions are made, They will also determine what is important (and what is not important) and in what order decisions are to be made.

In his book *Values Driven Leadership*, Aubrey Malphurs describes the importance of values this way: "The ministry that develops a clear set of values, shared by the ministry team, will make better decisions than the ones that have not developed their values set. They will clearly understand and share why they have done what they have done."[12] Teams that have not intentionally developed clear values tend to make decisions on a whim based largely on emotions.

When values have not been intentionally developed, there is the imminent danger of giving in to the "just this once" temptation. This can lead down a dangerous path that has caused havoc and heartache in many churches and in personal lives throughout the years. Without clear values, we can allow our emotions to guide us—and our emotions can change on a whim, allowing us to drift off course (e.g., see Acts 6:1–5). Each team member (staff and volunteer) at Saddleback Church is asked to fully commit to our team values before they are approved to work with children at our church.

Saddleback Kids' Team Values

Team values differ from church to church. The big idea is not for you to adopt a certain list of values, but rather to develop a set of team values that will act as a guide to keep you on track with the vision of your children's ministry.

The five values of our children's ministry at Saddleback Church can serve as an example:

1. Safety and Security—Protecting children is our number one value! Matthew 18:6 ICB
2. Teamwork—Serving together lightens the load and strengthens the heart. Ecclesiastes 4:9–12 NIV
3. Adaptability—The ability to be flexible in a changing culture or environment for the sake of the team and the big picture. Romans 12:1–2 CEV
4. Relevance—Being aware of your culture and being willing to adapt in order to effectively communicate and connect with your audience. 1 Corinthians 9:22 NLT
5. Shepherd Leadership—Leading others in the leadership style modeled by Christ. Psalm 78:72 NLT

Vision Statement. Some people question the necessity of a vision statement for those who already have a mission statement.

I don't blame anyone for asking that question as I have wondered the same thing. My ministry has both a mission statement and a vision statement, and at one point I actually considered dropping the vision statement until I understood the partnership between the two. To understand this partnership, we must first be clear on the definitions of the two and how they function.

Look straight ahead, and fix your eyes on what lies before you.

(PROVERBS 4:25 NLT)

As you recall, the mission statement is a brief but complete description of the overall purpose for your ministry. It answers the question "Why do we exist?" As an example, here is the mission statement for the children's ministry at Saddleback Church:

> The children's ministry at Saddleback Church exists to bring children into age-appropriate WORSHIP where they can BELONG to the family of God, GROW in their relationship with Christ, learn to SERVE, and then go SHARE Christ in the world.

The mission statement is the foundation of the entire ministry structure as the one component that does not and will not change.

The vision statement is a clear and simplified picture of the mission statement in action.

This clear and simplified picture of the mission statement is a motivating "battle cry" that people can rally around. The vision statement reminds your team why they do what they do. So, what would a clear and simplified picture of our purpose statement look like?

Our vision statement for the children's ministry at Saddleback Church is: "Connect kids to God and others."

When I ask one of our volunteers, "What are we going to do today," they immediately respond, "Connect kids to God and others." This is a clear and simplified picture of our overall purpose that is reflected in our mission statement. The image of moving kids toward spiritual health as described in the mission statement is "Connecting kids to God and others."

While it's easy to understand the importance of connecting kids to God, here's why we include in the vision connecting kids to other kids. One Sunday a fifth-grade girl named Brooke attended one of our weekend services at Saddleback Church for the first time. As you might expect any new girl to react in a new environment, Brooke checked in, walked inside, and sat down in the back by herself. She remained there until her parents picked her up at the end of the service.

Personally, I was on cloud nine that day. We had just led one of our better services—the worship was awesome, the games connected well, and the kids had tuned in to the teaching. In my mind, we had knocked that weekend service out of the park. So you can imagine what I was expecting to hear from Brooke's mom when she pulled me aside after the service. I thought I'd be thanked with encouraging affirmations, such as, "Oh, Brooke loved the service today and can't wait to come back!" But no, that is not what I heard. Not at all.

Here's what Brooke's mom said, "Excuse me, they said you're the pastor. Is that correct?" I replied, "Yes, I am." She looked me in the eyes and asked, "This was Brooke's first time here, and she said it was terrible and that she doesn't want to come back. Can you help me understand what happened?"

I discovered that Brooke actually liked the service. She told her mom she "hated it" because, in her words, "no one talked to me." That wasn't the first time I experienced a scenario like this, but in that moment, I wanted it to be the last.

The vision statement gives us a simple picture of not only what must be done but also what is being done in the moment ... connect kids to God and others. If we don't connect kids to other kids, we will eventually lose the opportunity to connect them to God. The vision statement keeps that reality in front of us. In Brooke's situation, we carelessly neglected one half of the equation, and it prevented us from having another opportunity to connect her to God in a weekend worship service.

Our volunteers may not be able to quote the strategy, structure, and process verbatim, and they may not remember every one of the values, but they can tell you our Vision Statement. Why? Because we intentionally repeat it as often as possible. I want them to visualize the mission statement in action and their contribution to the mission.

Your children's ministry has a specific purpose. Along with the purpose, God has provided the potential to accomplish the mission he has destined for every children's ministry. Developing a strategy for leading kids toward spiritual health and establishing a structure with the components necessary to support the strategy will move your ministry one step closer to fulfilling its full potential.

Now that we've identified the what—our structure—I would like to take a deeper look at one of the most crucial components to that structure—volunteers!

Visit www.childrensministryonpurpose.com to download the free discussion guide with reflection questions and activities for Chapter 7. These activities and questions will help you think through the essential components that must be in place to support your strategy, develop a clear structure for your ministry, understand the importance of Team Values and how to develop them, and then learn to communicate your team's core values.

CHAPTER 8

Developing a Healthy Volunteer Team

I'm going to let you in on a little secret: The greatest resource, or asset, at Saddleback Church is our volunteer team members. If you want to see excellence, commitment, and dedication, visit a Saddleback Church campus and watch our volunteer team. Every week, regardless of the pathway or program they are leading, our volunteers serve with joy, and I'm honored to serve with them. They are the reason our ministry has been effective in our mission to move kids toward spiritual health. So I'd like to let you in on what I've learned about healthy teams. This doesn't mean we don't have issues to work through every now and again, because issues do come up. We've learned a lot along our journey.

The volunteers' outstanding performance didn't happen automatically. It's the result of multiple factors working together. Pastor Rick establishes an expectation for those who call Saddleback their church home to use their talents as worship to the Lord. Another factor is that we have world-class children's ministry staff members who love and care for our volunteer team. Those and other factors contribute to a healthy serving environment that produces healthy serving experiences. The goal of this chapter is to examine purposeful steps children's ministry leaders can take to move toward creating healthy environments and healthy experiences for volunteers who serve.

With regard to the health of a ministry team, recall the connection I made earlier to physical health. Coming back to this analogy will help us better understand the nature of a healthy ministry. Before seeing a doctor, it's common to be asked to complete several forms that ask for personal information, family health history, and questions about your current health and your reason for seeing the doctor. It's not exhaustive and certainly can't be used to give a diagnosis. It's just a small tool the doctor uses to get a quick glimpse of your current health. Before we talk about the volunteers who serve on your team, I thought it would be helpful to do a similar exercise as it relates to the health of volunteer teams.

As I said earlier in the book, it takes a healthy children's ministry to lead kids toward spiritual health. But you cannot have a healthy ministry without a healthy volunteer team. I don't claim to offer every answer you need for building and developing a healthy volunteer team. I do believe, however, that the information here will either provide you with an effective framework for improving the health of your volunteer team or it will help guide your thoughts to discover the framework that is right for your ministry.

Building a Healthy Volunteer Team

Have you ever walked through your church and had the sense that people were avoiding you? Have you ever tried to simply say "hi" to someone at church, and the moment you approach they start giving you reasons why they have to say no even though you weren't going to ask them anything? Have you ever found yourself so desperate for volunteers that you were willing to take any living human being?

If so, then welcome to children's ministry. We've all been there. Enlisting volunteer team members is an ongoing process that seems to never end. It can be discouraging. I don't offer this information as a "one size fits all" approach to building volunteer teams. It's what I have learned over the years and what has worked well in creating healthy serving environments so volunteers have healthy serving experiences.

For a time recruiting volunteers was one of my least favorite responsibilities. There seemed to be a mutual dislike of the process among the people I was trying to recruit. I didn't want to talk to them about volunteering, and they didn't want me talking to them about volunteering either. But that all changed one day when God opened my eyes to help me fully understand a certain truth. This experience forever changed my perspective on building volunteer teams.

This experience was rooted in a Bible passage: "God has given each of you a gift from his great variety of spiritual gifts. Use them well to serve one another" (1 Peter 4:10 NLT).

I had read this verse before, but on this particular occasion, God revealed a deeper understanding that altered my perspective of volunteers. My revelation was this: Every person in my church has a gift, whether I can see the evidence of that gift or not, and God expects each person to utilize or manage those gifts so he can fully bless them.

Suddenly, I didn't see the volunteer needs in my ministry as merely "open slots"; instead, I saw them as opportunities for God's people to exercise their gifts. God gave gifts to them, and he wants them to receive the blessing that comes from using those gifts. My attitude shifted from seeing this as a burdensome task to a joyous privilege. So I encourage you: Don't see yourself as a recruiter, see yourself as a talent scout.

Volunteer Talent Scout, Not Volunteer Recruiter

Talent scouts can be found in almost any profession. Their job is to identify people with specific or unique talents and then convince that person to join their team. Successful talent scouts are very perceptive and constantly on the lookout for those individuals who unknowingly possess desirable or sought-after skills.

As Jesus began building the team that would serve alongside him, he took the time to discover the individuals his team needed. Jesus approached Peter and Andrew as a talent scout, not as a volunteer recruiter, and that made all the difference in their ministry in the years to come. We see this principle at work when Jesus called some of his disciples to follow him.

As Jesus was walking beside the Sea of Galilee, he saw two brothers, Simon called Peter and his brother Andrew. They were casting a net into the lake, for they were fishermen. "Come, follow me," Jesus said, "and I will send you out to fish for people." At once they left their nets and followed him.

Going on from there, he saw two other brothers, James son of Zebedee and his brother John. They were in a boat with their father Zebedee, preparing their nets. Jesus called them, and immediately they left the boat and their father and followed him.

MATTHEW 4:18–22

177

Jesus had been purposefully observing these men and could see that they possessed the skills he was looking for. Once he discovered their talent, he offered them an opportunity to use that talent on a "bigger stage."

Like Jesus, we must be intentional about discovering the talent around us. For most people, the area around us is our church. In Matthew 4, Jesus wasn't walking around that lake randomly and just happened to come across the guys who would become his disciples. He was there for a reason. This was not Jesus' first encounter with these guys. He had been observing them and had been thinking about how they could add value to his team. Jesus obviously could see they were fishermen by trade, but he saw much more than that. He saw two guys who could change the world.

Is it possible that there are talented people walking around in your church who have yet to be discovered? Before I experienced this shift in my perspective, I viewed people who were not volunteering as either too busy to serve, not qualified, overqualified, or simply lazy. But now I saw them as gifted talent who needed a stage to express their gift. There was just one problem. I was so busy during Sunday morning services, I didn't have time to scout the talent. So I developed a small team of volunteers who had one primary responsibility—to find new volunteers who are gifted in children's ministry. Guess what I called them. If you guessed Children's Ministry Talent Scouts, you are right. At times we would post them at the doors as greeters, and other times they would just walk around the church and talk with people with the goal of discovering potential volunteer team members.

The big idea is to see the people in your church as "performers in need of a stage." They are God's masterpiece creation uniquely and purposefully gifted to participate in advancing the kingdom of God (see Eph. 2:10). See yourself as a talent scout. Discover the gifted people in your church and find ways to utilize their gifts.

A few vital tips to remember as you are scouting the talent around you. First, do not make assumptions about people's availability or commitment level. Do not say no for people. Let them do that. This is another mistake I made many times. Because people are busy, I don't like to bother them and add one more thing to their plate. I thought I was being considerate. Until one day I was talking to one of those incredibly talented individuals that any leader would love to have on their team. During our conversation, he told me how he altered his work schedule so he could serve every week in the ministry he was currently a part of. I hinted that I wished we could have gotten him involved in children's ministry. He responded, "I would have jumped at the chance to serve in children's ministry, but I didn't think you guys wanted me."

Wow. I had assumed he was too busy, and he assumed we didn't want him. Don't say no for people. Present the opportunity and leave the rest to them and God.

As you take steps to build your volunteer team, be intentional about targeting men. In no way am I hinting that men are more vital than women or that you should not be considerate of women when enlisting volunteers. The point I am making is this—for as long as I can remember, women have carried the bulk of the load in children's ministry . . . and thank God they did! But a healthy team needs men and women to journey with our kids as they navigate the landscape of life and move toward spiritual health.

We have a great need for men in children's ministry. How do we effectively target men? Here are a few ideas:

1. When you create any type of marketing for your
   ministry, design it to be appealing to men. A manly
   looking promotional doesn't usually affect a woman's
   decision to get involved or not. However, if you hand a
   man a cute flyer with flowers and pretty lettering on the
   front, he will *instantly* think, "This is for women" and
   dismiss it.

2. Find ways to reinforce the importance and significance
   of children's ministry with the men in your church. Help
   them to understand how vital it is for men to model
   serving for the boys in your church.

3. Redefine the stereotype of a children's ministry
   volunteer in your church culture. Find ways to make
   your children's ministry appealing to men and honor the
   men who are serving.

Another element to remember while scouting talent is to
strategically and purposefully enlist teenagers. We call the teenagers who serve in our children's ministry "Student Leaders," and I
honestly can't imagine doing our ministry without them. We have
a strategic partnership with the leaders of our Student Ministries
Department to provide serving opportunities for our teenagers to
both benefit the children's ministry and build into the spiritual
growth and development of the teenager. If you have experienced
difficulty in utilizing teenagers in your children's ministry, I would
strongly encourage you to think through a new approach to involve
them in your children's ministry. We don't use Student Leaders to
just "fill a gap." Their contribution to the strategy and the serving
environment go much, much deeper than that.

As I said before in chapter 6, young people who serve

consistently have a greater likelihood of remaining engaged in the local church than those who do not serve. For that reason alone, I'll make up jobs in my ministry if that's what I have to do to keep students involved.

Why do we use students as volunteers in our children's ministry? When a student leader walks into the room, they are instantly the most influential person present. They command instant attention from the kids because of the cool factor. Let's be honest about this. In the eyes of the kids, the student leaders are way cooler than us adults. Also, student leaders increase the level of energy. Student leaders probably are more willing to get on the floor with the kids!

It's important that the strategy you develop for utilizing teenagers is developed in conjunction with the Youth Department. The serving opportunities in your ministry should never compete with the teenager's involvement in their youth ministry services or events.

The Enlistment Conversation

Okay, you have been watching people in your church, trying to discover the next "world's greatest volunteer," and you found a potential team member. Now what? Here are some proven methods for the enlistment conversation with a potential team member that Jesus modeled in his enlistment process.

1. Talk to potential volunteer team members face-to-face.

Again, this may seem a little obvious, but too many times we rely on things like announcements in the adult service, request for "help" in the church bulletin, or a posted sign-up sheet.

These things are impersonal and can send the wrong message. Research has proven that the majority of people who volunteer will do so because someone asked them in a face-to-face conversation.

2. Challenge people to invest their time and gifts in kingdom work.

When Jesus approached Peter and Andrew, he offered those guys a challenge to do something significant with their life.

"Come, follow me," Jesus said, "and I will send you out to fish for people."

He didn't say, "Come with me if you have time." He said, "Come, follow me, and I will show you how to fish for people!" (NLT). He wasn't apologetic, and he didn't sugarcoat it. He simply said, Hey if you want more out of life, come with me and I'll show you how to make an impact on this world that you couldn't dream possible sitting in those boats. It will require sacrifice and full commitment, but it's worth it. After all, this is kingdom work.

"You get the best effort from others not by lighting a fire beneath them, but by building a fire within them," is from Bill Hewlett, cofounder of Hewlett-Packard.

People want to be challenged because a challenge brings out the best in all of us.

3. Inspire potential team members with a vision, not a plea for help.

People want to work for a "cause," not just a living. They want to be a part of something that is making a difference. Remember what I said earlier: no one wants to jump onboard a sinking ship. A plea for help or begging for help says, "We are sinking and we'll take anyone who wants to go down with the ship." However, when you approach a potential volunteer with a vision, it paints a picture of eternal impact and enables them to visualize themselves being a part it. Jesus shared a vision that was inspirational enough for men to leave a profitable fishing business and trade financial and professional security for an unknown future.

"At once they left their nets and followed him." Jesus had a vision and knew how these men would play a part in that vision.

- He knew where he was going.
- He knew how he was going to get there.
- He knew what he needed from the team.

If the leader doesn't have a clear vision for the ministry, it's easy to fall into the trap of using guilt as a motivator. And while this may work in the short term, it does not work for the long term and will eventually hurt your ministry.

4. When communicating to potential volunteer team members, display confidence and faith in your ministry.

The Scripture isn't clear exactly how Jesus approached these guys, but one thing is clear, he was confident in his mission and vision. He was so confident in his mission that he was willing to present the vision at the most inopportune time. In Luke 5, Peter and James had just finished a long night of fishing and were cleaning their nets. They had caught nothing all night. They were tired and frustrated. They had nothing to show for a long night's work. But none of these factors prevented Jesus from offering them a chance to change the world because he had confidence in his ministry.

5. Be upfront and honest about the commitment you are looking for.

From the beginning, Peter and Andrew knew what it would cost them. The calling Jesus gave them came with a price. They had to drop everything and follow him. By Jesus saying, "Come, follow me," Peter and Andrew knew this was not a casual invitation. This was a commitment to literally follow Jesus everywhere and accept the responsibilities and sacrifices required to be someone's disciple.

Now, not every believer is given that same level of calling. But regardless of the level of your calling, it does come with a price, and Jesus was clear what that price would be. The higher the level of ministry, the higher the calling, the greater the sacrifice. It will cost you something.

You and your team members will invest time, effort, and energy. Different roles in ministry require different levels of investment, but even on the smallest level, there is a cost, and Jesus made that cost clear. He was up front and honest about the roles and responsibilities, expectations and requirements, and we must do the same.

Onboarding

There are several important steps to follow when enlisting volunteers to keep the safety and security of your kids, volunteers, and church a priority. Here I will walk you through what the volunteer approval process for the children's ministry at Saddleback Church looks like. Your church's process may look different and that's totally okay. This is simply a guide.

In the onboarding process, we have an opportunity to establish a relationship with each potential volunteer team member and assist them in discovering which area of our ministry is the best fit for them and the team. This process begins with our "Saddleback Kids Orientation," where we introduce them to our ministry and clearly present the following information:

- The requirements to be a team member in our ministry.
- The church's statement of faith.
- The strategy and structure of our ministry.
- Our mission, vision, and values.
- The expectations of each team member regarding attitude, teamwork, and commitment.
- General policies.
- Next steps in the process.

Every potential volunteer is required to complete an application, provide references, and complete a background check. Once the potential volunteer has attended orientation and filled out the application, a children's ministry coordinator schedules a personal interview with the candidate. This is a forty-five-minute interview conducted by a member of the children's ministry staff. During the interview, one of the objectives is to discover the best serving opportunity for the volunteer based on their gifts, personality, and preferences. One of the keys to creating a healthy serving environment that produces healthy serving experiences is to let volunteers serve in areas that utilize their strengths, passions, and interests. Once its determined what area of children's ministry the volunteer will be serving, we then communicate the role and responsibilities of that specific area.

Developing a Healthy Volunteer Team

Now that you have enlisted new team members and taken them through the onboarding process, it's imperative to continually develop them through intentional equipping, empowerment, and encouragement.

These are the gifts Christ gave to the church: the apostles, the prophets, the evangelists, and the pastors and teachers. Their responsibility is to equip God's people to do his work and build up the church, the body of Christ.

EPHESIANS 4:11–12 NLT

Equipping

In his book *LeaderShift*, Don Cousins defines leadership this way: "If you hold a leadership position but are not equipping the saints for the work of service, then you are not a leader. You may hold the position; you may have the title; you may be called a leader; but you're not a leader as the Bible defines it, because leadership means equipping."[13]

Here's how I define equipping for ministry teams: Equipping is the ongoing process of intentionally and strategically preparing your team members to succeed in their ministry role by developing their skills.

Whether you use the word "training" or "equipping" to represent this process is a matter of preference. The important thing is that it's actually happening in your ministry. The definition I coined for equipping gives us the big-picture view of what needs to be done but doesn't specify how it should be done. I want to focus your attention on the important elements of equipping. Keep these in mind as you build your team:

- *Be intentional and strategic.* I'm sure you have noticed that I use the words "intentional" and "strategic" a lot. Those two words are inseparable from the purpose driven approach. If it's not intentional, then it's random; and if it's not strategic, then it happens in isolation. To effectively "equip God's people to do his work and build up the church," there must be an intentional plan that has been strategically designed and scheduled. Having a well-thought-out intentional plan for equipping your volunteers throughout the ministry season is doable and necessary if you want to create a healthy serving environment.

- *Prepare your team to succeed in their ministry role.* God invested gifts and talents in every person. As church leaders, our job is to prepare those we lead to succeed in their mission and calling. When the volunteer team member succeeds, your ministry succeeds, which means the kids win. If a team member is not succeeding in their role at my church, I first ask myself if we gave that team member what they needed to succeed.

- *Develop their skills.* I doubt there are many volunteer team members in your ministry who wake up each day and think, I hope I don't learn one thing today. In fact, I hope I fail at whatever I do. I realize this is a ridiculous example, because no one in their right mind feels this way. We all want to succeed and we all have a desire to grow and perform well. People who are not super passionate about growth, improvement, or development still have a desire and a need to be successful on some level.

Jesus shows us the importance of equipping and leadership training. Jesus shows us how to scout talent. He displays the heart of an equipper. Think of the time Jesus enlisted fishermen for his team. I made the statement in chapter 2 that Jesus was purposeful in everything he did. And we hear a strong sense of purpose in this statement: "Come, follow me, and I will show you how to fish for people!" (Matt. 4:19 NLT). Jesus had a plan. He knew these guys had potential and skills, but their skills had to be developed for their potential to be realized. Jesus was purposeful in equipping his new team.

As with most things, there is no single way to equip volunteer team members. How the equipping is done—where it happens, when it happens, how the training is delivered—and the content of the training should all be tailored to the culture of your church and your church strategy.

Just to kick-start your thinking and maybe spark some new and creative approaches you can take to the equipping process in your ministry, I'll give a brief overview of the equipping structure we use in Saddleback's children's ministry.

I refer to our calendar year as a ministry season, which runs January through December. For each ministry season, our children's ministry follows a theme. We use ministry themes for two primary reasons: to create alignment and bring focus to our team. I determine the theme and develop that theme to teach, train, and encourage our team members throughout the year. The theme is designed to equip paid and volunteer team members. This equipping plan and process involves weekly connections in our Pre-Game meeting thirty minutes before the start of each service, monthly training, age (or grade) level training, quarterly training, and our annual gathering to kick off the new ministry season.

Empowering the Volunteer Team

Jesus called his twelve disciples together and gave them authority to cast out evil spirits and to heal every kind of disease and illness.

MATTHEW 10:1 NLT

Once you enlist volunteer team members and begin the equipping process with them, you must empower them to fulfill their role and responsibilities. Here's my definition of empowering volunteers for ministry: Empowering is providing the opportunity and environment that enables a team member to effectively exercise their gifts within their role.

But how do we empower volunteers? I offer five tips for how to do this.

First, empower volunteers by releasing them to do their job. Once they have been trained, allow them to do what they are there to do. Allow them to make mistakes by avoiding the mentality that says, "No one else can do it the way I want it done." Train your volunteer team members, then release them to do what you trained them to do while you continue to partner with them through training.

Second, empower volunteers by giving them the opportunity to give input and share ideas.

If your team members have a brain, they have ideas. If you have five people in a room, is it better to utilize one brain or all five? Well, I guess that depends on who is in the room. However, it is wrong for me to think that I am the only one who has good ideas. That kind of thinking is rooted in pride and arrogance. Good leaders know how to mine ideas from their team. In doing so, we make volunteers feel valued because they have been heard.

Third, empower your team by clearly communicating to them with accurate information. In chapter 7, I talked about communication channels being an essential component to the structure of your children's ministry as they contribute to the health of the serving environment. Clear and accurate information distributed through effective communication channels will empower your volunteer team members by reducing confusion. For example, when people have only part of the information, they will make assumptions about the information they don't have. After a while, the actual communication and the assumptions blend into an incorrect message that will confuse others as it is passed along in conversations with other team members.

Clear communication also creates synergy. Good communication creates synergy by creating excitement and momentum with the individual team members through their conversations. Solid communication also creates connectedness. Everyone wants to be in the know, and no one wants to be on the outside looking in. When we communicate clear and accurate information to the volunteer team members, they feel connected to your ministry on a personal level.

Fourth, I tell ministry leaders to empower their team members by providing them with the resources and teaching tools necessary to successfully implement the strategy. Think of it like this—If you need to drive a nail into a piece of wood, you are not going to pick up a handsaw. If you do, you're only going to be frustrated because the saw is not designed to drive nails into wood. To successfully complete your project, you not only need the proper materials, you need the proper tools. I realize we can't always provide the ideal resources, but it's important to do the best we can to provide the teaching tools and resources our volunteers need to implement the strategy.

Last, I advise people to empower volunteers by providing new opportunities to grow and express their leadership abilities. While all volunteer team members are leaders, you will notice that some have stronger and more natural leadership abilities and tendencies than others. At Saddleback, we empower volunteer leaders like this by expanding their leadership influence in our children's ministry in a position we call a "coach."

The position of coach is the highest level of volunteer leadership in our children's ministry. These team members are the key leaders for each of our programs and are an essential component to successfully implementing our strategy. They have a deep understanding of our ministry strategy, structure, and DNA and are highly committed to serving in our ministry. Our coaches basically "run the show" for each program. The paid staff work directly with the coach and support them as they lead and support the other volunteers and ensure the program is running smoothly.

The coaches in our children's ministry have made such a positive impact that I highly encourage you to implement a volunteer leadership position like this in your ministry. Without the coaches, our children's ministry would not function at the level of excellence we experience each week.

Encouraging the Volunteer Team

Let us think of ways to motivate one another to acts of love and good works.

HEBREWS 10:24 NLT

I love to be encouraged, don't you? There have been times that one simple encouragement offered at the right time was all I needed to get through a difficult day or circumstance. It's easy to underestimate the power of simple encouragement. Yet we all need and want to be encouraged, valued, and appreciated.

How do we encourage our volunteer team members? It's simple: through recognition and appreciation. As you recognize your volunteers, point out how their efforts make a difference and exactly how they contribute to the kingdom. Then remind people that they are gifted and that their gifts are needed in your ministry. As you appreciate your team members, point out their time, sacrifice, passion, and commitment. Here's how it works:

Recognition + Appreciation = Encouragement

One of our volunteers who serves at our weekend service recently shared a story with me that perfectly illustrates the power of encouragement. She has served in children's ministry for over eight years and has loved every minute. But this ministry season was different. Her passion level was not as strong as it had been in the past, her energy level was lower than normal, the kids in her class were more challenging than she had ever experienced, and she had lost confidence in her ability to make a difference with the kids. It was the perfect storm of despair. During the middle of the ministry hour, she made the decision to quit children's ministry and intended to let her coordinator know at the conclusion of the service. She taught the lesson and got through the morning, but this would be her last one. After all the kids were picked up, she began resetting the room for the next service and finalizing her verbal resignation in her mind. Suddenly, a mom came into the room and said, "I have been meaning to do this for weeks, I just wanted to let you know our son loves your class and refuses to miss a single Sunday. He's not the easiest child to work with, trust me, we know that, but whatever you are doing is working. On the way home every Sunday, he tells us all about his class and the lesson you taught. You should know that we made this our church home because he loves your class so much. Thank you." One encouraging word overshadowed multiple levels of despair, reminded this volunteer of her calling, and rekindled dwindling passion.

This is one of the most powerful tools at your disposal, so use it generously. However, while it's important to use it generously, it's even more important to use it wisely. Let me explain what I mean by that. It's not possible for me to know every one of my volunteer team members because Saddleback Church has many campuses spread out across the globe. And while I don't have a deep personal relationship with each volunteer, I still have a sincere appreciation for them personally and for the part they play in leading our kids toward spiritual health. I don't have to know them personally to recognize their efforts and show authentic appreciation for their involvement in children's ministry. But if the recognition and appreciation I am giving is rooted in anything other than genuine love and a kindred spirit, it can quickly feel like shallow compliments. If your team members have this perspective of your encouragements, it will backfire and you eventually will have done more harm than good.

As your relationship deepens with each volunteer, you'll be poised to offer specific encouragement. Recognize and appreciate your volunteers for not only what they do but for who they are. As Paul said to the Thessalonians: "Encourage each other and build each other up, just as you are already doing" (1 Thess. 5:11 NLT).

As I mentioned at the beginning of this chapter, volunteers are your most vital resource in children's ministry. Take the right time to nurture them, equip them, and keep them on your team. This requires structure and strategy, but in the end the time you spend figuring these out on the front end will pay dividends for years to come. Your team members—paid or unpaid—will thank you. Your senior pastor will thank you. The children will even thank you (in their own way).

It's good to remember that there is no such thing as the perfect "system" or "process." If everything had to be perfect before we implemented it, we would get nothing done. Ecclesiastes 11:4 tells us that if you wait for perfect conditions, you will never get anything done (my translation). That's true of people as well. People, no matter how committed, called, and passionate they may be about children's ministry, have flaws that are sometimes revealed in conflict. Conflict is a natural feature of being human and being a part of a team. The question is not whether your team has conflict, the question is what kind of conflict—healthy conflict or unhealthy conflict. Because of this, you will have volunteers quit from time to time, and you may find yourself in a situation where you have to dismiss a volunteer. The goal is not to eliminate conflict, but to realize it's natural and there are healthy ways to deal with conflict.

By taking care of your volunteers, you honor God and disciple them in the ways of Jesus. In fact, the way that you care for your leaders will trickle down to how they care for the kids in your ministry. That's just how it works. So take the time you need to properly structure your volunteer base to create healthy serving environments that produce healthy serving experiences. By doing so, you enable your ministry to grow and develop to its full potential as you lead kids toward spiritual health.

Ultimately, the kind of leader you are will translate into the types of leaders you raise up. That's why I have devoted the next chapter to becoming the type of leader people will follow.

Visit www.childrensministryonpurpose.com to download the free discussion guide with reflection questions and activities for Chapter 8. These activities and questions will help you to process whether you have a healthy serving environment that produces healthy serving experiences. You'll find a health indicator test for your ministry volunteers and will work through the critical components to the process that will enable you to more effectively build, develop and lead a healthy volunteer team. And you'll find several resources for helping you onboard, enlist, and train your team of volunteers including advice on how to lead effective training sessions, the responsibilities and requirements of a coach, and how to deal with conflict in ministry.

CHAPTER 9

Becoming a Leader
People Will Follow

Just like caring for volunteers is vital to your ministry, so is caring for yourself. We move from thinking purposefully and strategically to thinking personally. This chapter is important for your ministry because I will discuss more personal matters. If you'll go there with me, God may have some things to reveal to you about your character, calling, and skills as a minister of the gospel. Who you are as a leader—many elements of which seem intangible—are just as important as what we've addressed thus far in the book.

I bring up this subject because there seems to be a limitless number of resources dedicated to the subject of leadership with an equal number of opinions and perspectives. We'll begin our discussion on leadership with this foundational axiom: Your ability to lead begins with your ability to follow. Let me say it another way: You will not lead well until you can follow well. Learning the art of following can be challenging, but when a leader is difficult to follow, it's even more challenging. Whether you follow someone by choice or obligation, you will always be following a leader.

Take a moment and think about the leader you are currently following. If given a way out, would you continue to choose them as your leader? Could you say of that leader, "I'll follow them anywhere"? Then consider your leadership. What would people say of you? I would like to challenge you to become the kind of leader that others willfully follow with the proclamation, "I'll follow that leader anywhere!"

King David As a Model Leader

What kind of leader will people follow? I believe the answer is found in the life and leadership of David. Years ago, while reading in the book of Psalms, I came across a verse that has become my definition of leadership, and I want to share it with you. This became my personal goal each and every day as I fulfill my calling as a leader in children's ministry. It comes from a description of David in Psalm 78:70–72 NLT:

> He chose his servant David, calling him from the sheep pens.
> He took David from tending the ewes and lambs and made
> him the shepherd of Jacob's descendants—God's own people,
> Israel. He cared for them with a true heart and led them with
> skillful hands.

From this, I discerned that to be a leader others will follow, I must:

- Care for them with a true heart and
- Lead them with skillful hands.

These are the primary elements of servant leadership. While I aim for these every day, some days I miss the mark and fail to implement some aspect of a caring heart or skillful hands. Yet this vision remains my goal, and I diligently target this goal every day. In this chapter, I want to develop this idea by sharing more with you on the calling, character, and competence of a leader, all within the context of a leader who has a caring heart. I'll use the life of David as a framework for each of these. His story begins when he was an unimpressive individual living an uneventful life.

A Leader's Calling

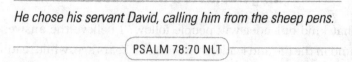

He chose his servant David, calling him from the sheep pens.

PSALM 78:70 NLT

Before David started his ministry as King of Israel, he was faithfully doing what he did best—taking care of sheep. One day when he was out in the fields, a messenger came running to him and said, "David, you have to come with me, the prophet Samuel, your father, and your brothers are waiting for you. They want to see you right now!" David scrambled to situate the sheep so he could leave. He rushed off to join his family, undoubtedly wondering what was going on.

The prophet Samuel had been instructed by God to find this man Jesse, David's father, and anoint one of his sons as the new king of Israel. (Read 1 Samuel 1–8 for the context of Israel before this point.) While David was out in the fields working, David's father, Jesse, was parading David's brothers one by one so Samuel could find who would be the next king of Israel. As each son came into the room, Samuel thought, This must be the one, but God said no.

But the Lord told him, "Samuel, don't think Eliab is the one just because he's tall and handsome. He isn't the one I've chosen. People judge others by what they look like, but I judge people by what is in their hearts."

1 SAMUEL 16:7 CEV

Each of Jesse's sons were presented to Samuel with the same result: "This is not the one the Lord has chosen." Finally, Samuel asked Jesse the key question: "Are these all the sons you have?" (1 Sam. 16:11 NLT).

Jesse's response tells us how lowly regarded David was in his own family: "There is still the youngest," Jesse replied. "But he's out in the fields watching the sheep and goats." "Send for him at once," Samuel said. "We will not sit down to eat until he arrives" (1 Sam. 16:11 NLT). Samuel was there to perform a sacrifice ceremony with Jesse and his sons, select one of the sons as the new king, and then have a feast. But no one in David's family thought to include him in the sacrifice, the selection process, or the feast. He was invited only because Samuel instructed Jesse to invite him. He was literally the odd man out.

When David finally arrived at the party, God spoke to Samuel: "'Anoint him; this is the one.' So as David stood there among his brothers, Samuel took the horn of oil and anointed David (1 Sam. 16:12–13). This was King David's calling.

God saw a heart that was truly his and hands that were capable and willing to be developed. David experienced a defining moment as Samuel poured the anointing oil on David's head, signifying he was called and anointed as the new king of Israel.

And the Spirit of the LORD came powerfully upon David from that day on.

1 SAMUEL 16:13 NLT

God chose David; he did not "inherit" the position, or randomly stumble upon it. Nor did he make a play for the position because of the benefits it would bring. God saw something special in this shepherd and called him out. The same is true for you and me. In spite of our deficiencies and flaws, God has called and commissioned us to change the landscape of eternity through children's ministry. Your calling is an anchor that will hold you steady during the storms of life and ministry and prevent you from being dashed against the rocks of hardship or drift with the winds of compromise.

My dad, the Reverend Basil J. Adams, taught me many valuable lessons about ministry and leadership. One such lesson was the significance of calling. He said that a calling begins with a burden, a deep soulful heaviness placed within you by the Holy Spirit. It consumes your thinking, perspectives, and emotions, and you can't escape it until you act on it. That burden leads to a vision—not necessarily a supernatural vision, but rather a vivid picture of what could be and how God could use you to make a difference. That vision leads to commitment, the unwavering devotion and faithfulness that keeps one focused and directed regardless of circumstances and feelings. This is a calling. It comes from God for his reasons and for his purposes. Your calling is not predicated on the views and opinions or the qualifications others think you do or don't have. Your calling is a divine mission that aligns your passions, interests, and talents for eternal purposes. It's the beginning of your leadership journey, but it certainly isn't the end.

David's life would never be the same after his calling. Neither would history be the same as this unassuming and seemingly unqualified shepherd boy followed his call to lead. But David's next order of business was not to pack his things and move into the palace—he headed back to the fields not only to take care of the sheep but to start the next phase of his development as a leader—character development.

The Leader's Character Development

He took David from tending the ewes and lambs and made him the shepherd of Jacob's descendants—God's own people, Israel.

PSALM 78:71 NLT

David, through his calling and character development, exemplified the kind of leader that others will follow, a servant leader. Before a person can lead effectively, they must journey through a time of preparation called character development. And just as our individual purpose, design, and calling are unique, so is this preparation God uses to make us ready for the next stage in our development. A leader's character forms from the inside out.

Your character is the sum total of all the qualities, traits, and features that distinguish you as an individual.

In essence, it's what makes you, you. Your character is formed through a combination of experiences, struggles, passions, talent, upbringing, desires, failures, successes, and more. God develops leaders much the same as a person develops as a disciple of Christ—through a process. From birth to present day, God is continually developing and growing those he calls to lead as spiritual leaders through a process of preparation. Sometimes this process of preparation seems to drag along slowly, and we would prefer that God would speed things up and make it happen right now. God in his wisdom, however, takes his sweet time, and when the time is right, our opportunity is presented.

David, after being anointed and announced as the new King of Israel, had to go back out into the fields and tend the sheep for another fifteen years before he stepped into his leadership role!

David was called and chosen, but he was not ready to take the throne.

The development of David's character began in the fields but continued throughout his life. The same is true for you and me as our growth and development is a continual process. Our character is developed by utilizing lessons we have learned in the past and consistently implementing wisdom today. Step by step we incrementally become the person God wants us to become.

It appears that the fields and the demands of leading a flock of sheep provided a great training ground for the kind of leader God wanted. David learned to be patient and trust God as he waited a decade and a half after his anointing. He endured many discouraging obstacles before finally taking the throne. He also learned how to be still, quiet his soul, and listen to God. Imagine all the time he had out in the fields with only the sheep to talk to and God to worship and think about. He was given many opportunities to grow close to God, even in the midst of intense, life-threatening challenges.

For example, he learned to be courageous as he was often required to defend the sheep against predators. David learned how to build trust with people by building trust with the sheep who learned to know his voice. Moving the herds from one area to another safely required strategic thinking, which became a valuable asset for David when he had to lead the military into battle and be mindful of all the political components connected to ruling as king. Of all the leadership lessons David learned in the fields, one of the most powerful had to be the way a shepherd actually led the sheep—out in front.

David learned to lead his people from the front, modeling the way to go.

We can clearly see how God used the fields to prepare and develop David's character to be a servant leader. Regardless of your age or leadership experience, you are constantly in a process of development and preparation to become a leader others will follow—a servant leader.

We shouldn't discount our troubles, difficulties, and trials. They are the training ground God uses to prepare us, just as he did David, for the journey ahead. We must walk in total surrender, knowing the good shepherd is watching out for us and is grooming us for his purposes. When David was finally ready, God took him from leading, protecting, and providing for sheep to leading, protecting, and providing for Israel, his people. David's journey as a shepherd developed him into a leader worthy of God's call.

David's not the only person whose character was forged through difficulties. Moses was living and working in the desert for forty years before receiving his call from God to lead the Israelites. Joshua served Moses for forty years before he had his opportunity to lead. Ultimately, David's role as servant leader was perfected by Jesus, who came to earth as a servant leader: "For even the Son of Man came not to be served but to serve others and to give his life as a ransom for many" (Matt. 20:28 NLT). Jesus was the Son of God, but he wasn't excused from preparation. He was in training and development for thirty years before he began fulfilling his purpose as a leader.

How did David lead his people? David's leadership is summed up in one verse that gives us a great definition of a servant leader: "He cared for them with a true heart and led them with skillful hands" (Ps. 78:72 NLT).

Care for Them with a True Heart

He cared for them with a true heart.

PSALM 78:72 NLT

What specifically did God see in David that everyone else missed? God could see what was on the inside, so he knew those internal qualities would eventually materialize on the outside. Servant leadership starts with the heart, and God was looking for a man after his own heart (1 Sam. 13:13–14). David had a heart that was truly his. There are three things we see in David's life that contributed to him having a heart that was truly HIS: Humility, Integrity, Spirituality. Each of these leadership qualities are nonnegotiable for a Servant Leader.

A heart of humility begins with one's attitude. Scripture admonishes us to have the same mindset or attitude as Jesus: "In your relationships with one another, have the same mindset as Christ Jesus: Who, being in very nature God, did not consider equality with God something to be used to his own advantage" (Phil. 2:5–6). Humility is the realization and acceptance of the fact that we are totally dependent on God's love and mercy. It develops and grows through a stripping away of all self-sufficiency as you learn total dependence on God, presenting yourself to him as clay to be shaped and molded into God's image. A humble leader recognizes that their own strength is massively insufficient and without God they are capable of nothing. I like how Ken Blanchard described humility when he said, "Humility does not mean you think less of yourself, it means you think of yourself less."

Every leader needs to operate with confidence, but the confidence we have is in God and the power that flows from him through us. Confidence rooted in our self apart from God is pride and will lead to certain downfall.

God opposes the proud but gives grace to the humble.

JAMES 4:6 NLT

Humility is the key characteristic in servant leadership as it compels the leader to think of others above themselves. The servant leader puts the concerns of those he or she leads at the forefront of their mind and makes their well-being the top priority. They value and appreciate those they lead by taking a sincere interest in their lives (Phil. 2:3 NLT). Humility is serving others and developing a lifestyle of focusing on others rather than ourselves: "True greatness, true leadership, is found in giving yourself in service to others, not in coaxing or inducing others to serve you."[14]

Another aspect of a true heart, in my experience, is simply this: You cannot lead without integrity because without integrity no one will follow you. Integrity is not perfection, rather it's a lifelong pursuit of consistent authenticity between our actions and convictions. It's alignment between what we say and what we do. David was a man of integrity, but he certainly wasn't perfect. He was a man of integrity in that he authentically pursued a lifestyle of consistency with his actions and convictions. As the Proverb says, "The LORD detests people with crooked hearts, but he delights in those with integrity" (Prov. 11:20 NLT).

Leaders with integrity build trust and credibility with those they lead. Trust is a confidence that transcends circumstances.

It's an assurance that the ability, character, or strength of a person is reliable. I taught both my sons how to swim the same way: By standing in a swimming pool with them on the side of the pool. I put out my arms and told them to jump into my arms. It was scary for them both, but they did it because they trusted me. Even though they were afraid and had no idea what I was doing, they had confidence that I would catch them. That's trust. No relationship (personal or professional) can thrive without it. The integrity of a leader builds trust and credibility, which will fuel the confidence necessary for someone to follow them into unknown or unfamiliar territory.

The sobering fact that all leaders must remember is this: It takes years to build trust and a single moment to lose it. A person with integrity also gains the benefit of protection from the arrows of accusations, lies, and deception. Although the arrows may still come, the "integrity of good people" creates a sense of confidence and assurance because there is nothing to hide. A person who lacks integrity places themselves in harm's way due to their own actions. As the Proverb says, "People with integrity walk safely, but those who follow crooked paths will be exposed" (Prov. 10:9 NLT).

The last element that I see comprising a true heart is spirituality. This is not mystical or mysterious; it's not religious hierarchy; and it has nothing to do with living a perfect life. Being a spiritual person is having an authentic, dynamic, and thriving connection to the living God. David exemplified a heart of spirituality in his genuine love for God and longing to be in his presence. That love created a "thirst" to be connected to God because we long for or want to be with the ones we love.

As a deer gets thirsty for streams of water, I truly am thirsty for you, my God. In my heart, I am thirsty for you, the living God. When will I see your face?

PSALM 42:1–2 CEV

A spiritual leader has a thriving connection to God that aligns their heart with his. This connection is a deep relationship that develops much like any other relationship—with time. Time spent studying his Word, in prayer, and in silence waiting on God to hear his voice is vital for a servant leader. This alignment with the heart of God is what makes servant leadership truly spiritual and allows a leader to function with a greater sense of discernment and power as God's power flows through them.

A heart that is aligned with God's heart will have a desire to do what pleases him. (Phil. 2:13 NLT)

A heart that is aligned with God's heart wants to obey God and his word. (Acts 13:22 NLT)

A heart that is aligned with God's heart will break over the same things that break the heart of God. (Luke 19:41 NLT)

A heart that is aligned with God's heart will love and care for people like the good shepherd. (John 10:11–14 NLT)

You have heard it said, "People don't care how much you know until they know how much you care." When a leader authentically cares for others in love, that's what matters—nothing more, nothing less. Without genuine love, caring for people becomes a mere transaction, a list item to check off. Some leaders will "care" for people because of the "return on investment." In other words, the disingenuous leader will pretend to care for people for what they can get in return. This type of leadership is motivated by self-centeredness. A servant leader, however, loves the people they lead. That love is evident and nurtured through relationship. The shepherd leader takes a genuine interest in the lives of the people under his or her care. By doing so, the leader knows how to pray for the "flock" and has greater insight on how to effectively guide and protect them as they journey together.

Lead Them with Skillful Hands

Leadership starts with a caring heart but must be executed with skillful hands. The skillful hands of a leader represent not only natural abilities and giftings but also learned competencies that enable them to perform certain tasks. David's skillful hands enabled him to carry out whatever was required of him whether he was in the field, on the battleground, or in the palace. In this section we will explore several core skills that are nonnegotiable if you want to be a leader that others will follow. There are many other contextual skills that are specific to your children's ministry that can and should be learned to make yourself an indispensable contributor to your children's ministry and senior pastor, but here we will discuss only several crucial categories that are necessary to be a leader others will follow.

1. Communication Skills

It is extremely difficult to cast a vision or inspire others if you are unable to communicate effectively. Communication is more than just dispersing information; it's connecting with your audience. That audience may be a group of kids, parents, volunteers, or your senior pastor. Whether you are communicating with someone on the phone, social media, email, face-to-face, or in a large group setting, a leader's ability to communicate effectively will determine how successful they are leading others. While there are multiple styles of communicating, the goal is the same—to connect with an audience to inform, inspire, or influence. I like what John Maxwell said in *Everyone Communicates, Few Connect*, "Connecting is the ability to identify with people and relate to them in a way that increases your influence with them."[15]

2. People Skills

I had no idea that those early years as a child playing in the sandbox with other kids would be the practice field and critical indicator of an essential skill in leadership. Who knew that playing well with others would eventually develop into working well with others. The ability to work well with others is not a bonus feature for successful leaders, it's essential to your success as a leader.

People skills are a wide range of competencies and attributes that provide productive interactions with others. A leader with good people skills is able to effectively interact with a variety of people in a way that is mutually beneficial. This skill set embodies attributes such as emotional intelligence, active listening skills, and good judgment. Leaders with good people skills are sensitive to other people's needs and concerns, and they are willing to work in collaboration to find solutions and resolve conflicts.

3. Organizational Skills

There are many details, tasks, and moving parts in children's ministry that require coordination and arrangement. Without some level of organization skills, a children's ministry leader will be unable to manage the people, programs, and processes necessary to successfully achieve the team's objectives. One of the key aspects of organizational skills is the ability to identify all the different parts that make up your ministry and envisioning how each part functions with the others. Strategic planning, properly allocating resources, and attention to action steps are all functions of good organization.

4. Time and Energy Management Skills

You can't be everywhere at once, you can't do it all, and you can't be everything that others want you to be. Again, that sounds almost ridiculously obvious. But in an age of endless choices, options, and opportunities, leaders feel pressured into being at every function, being a part of every activity, or going to every event they are invited to because that's what effective leaders do, right? Wrong. Someone said to me a long time ago, "If you don't control your life and schedule, someone else will." It's true that we don't have the luxury of total freedom when it comes to our time and involvement in activities. So the focus must be on what you can control, not on what you can't control.

One of the lessons I learned over the years about maximizing time and energy is this—it comes down to prioritization and choice. And when a leader doesn't want to choose, they try to do it all and eventually burn themselves out and those around them. In his book *Essentialism*, Greg McKeown says, "Many capable people are kept from getting to the next level of contribution because they can't let go of the belief that everything is important."[16] Some of the things we consider to be important are simply routines we are unwilling or afraid to break out of. Busyness and activity do not necessarily equate accomplishment and production. In fact, busyness and excessive activity reduce production, effectiveness, and efficiency.

5. Team-Building Skills

It's impossible to lead with skillful hands without having the ability to build a team. Inspiring and motivating others to action is the first skill in team building. In her book *Multipliers*, Liz Wiseman identifies two types of leaders—Multipliers and Diminishers. Diminishers are those leaders who are so absorbed in their own talents and intelligence that they stifle the creativity, intelligence, and capabilities of the team around them. They are the "geniuses" with little to no regard for anyone else's ideas and have no interest in or intention of developing those around them. A Multiplier is a genius maker. They are committed to bringing out the best in those around them. "Because Multipliers are leaders who look beyond their own genius and focus their energy on extracting and extending the genius of others, they get more from their people. They don't get a little more; they get vastly more."[17]

Multipliers are leaders who go out of their way to identify people who have something to offer and enlist them on the team. They equip and empower them to reach their full potential while maintaining an environment that celebrates and encourages collective thought and teamwork.

6. Resourceful Skills

Resourcefulness is the ability to creatively cope and overcome difficulties and unusual problems. The skill of resourcefulness includes problem solving, innovative thinking, and decision making. The resourcefulness of a leader strengthens their ability to make quick decisions under pressure with limited information. One of the characteristics of a resourceful leader is the inclination and willingness to ask empowering questions. A resourceful thinker is willing to consider ideas and possibilities that less resourceful leaders will miss.

Good Leaders Are Good Followers

You've got a calling, character in formation, a caring heart, and skills for ministry. Those are the essentials that make a leader. All of these work themselves out in the context of real life, where you are not just a leader but a follower too. If you struggle to follow those who are leading you, it will affect how others follow you. There's no way around it.

Here is the scenario: You are sure of your calling in ministry, you feel confident that you are serving where God wants you to be, but you are finding it very difficult to follow your leader. So what do you do? There is a powerful principle in Galatians 6:7 that must be thoughtfully considered before we go any farther. It's called the seed-sowing principle: "Don't be misled—you cannot mock the justice of God. You will always harvest what you plant" (Gal. 6:7 NLT). The verse starts out "don't be misled." We cannot think that we can act one way toward our leader and expect those we lead to act any differently toward us. Your team will follow your leadership in the same manner you follow your leader. Your actions toward your leader will sow similar seeds into your own leadership.

As I have said many times, if you are going to fight for anything, fight for unity in the body of Christ. As Paul said to the

Ephesians: "Make every effort to keep yourselves united in the Spirit, binding yourselves together with peace" (Eph. 4:3 NLT).

It's not our job to change our leaders; it's our job to support the senior pastor and do what we can to make their job easier. This is a joy when we respect and appreciate our senior pastor's leadership. However, if you serve a senior pastor whose leadership is difficult to follow, life can feel challenging. It's usually not very hard to find others who are experiencing similar difficulties with senior leadership. While this can be a source of comfort knowing we are not alone, it can also be extremely dangerous if we are constantly "processing" the situation and obstacles with our comrades.

The same way you water and nurture a seed to grow a healthy plant, the more you talk and process the same difficulties about your leader, the more you will nurture the potential seeds of bitterness and discord. This will only make alignment and proper attitude that much more difficult to attain. I'm not suggesting that you keep all your frustrations bottled up inside as this can be dangerous for you personally. I merely make the point that constant processing about the same problems over and over will feed your frustration, highlight the struggles, and make it increasingly more difficult to overcome.

Watch the Condition of Your Heart

As leaders we have a responsibility to protect, guide, and feed those in our flocks, but we must also be mindful of our own internal well-being. We must watch out for the devious tactics of our enemy who, like a roaring lion, is stealth and cunning working under the cover of darkness, lurking about waiting for that moment we fall asleep or get distracted and then he attacks (see

1 Peter 5:8). Pay close attention to the first phrase of this passage, one that leaders can be tempted to overlook: "So guard yourselves and God's people. Feed and shepherd God's flock—his church, purchased with his own blood—over which the Holy Spirit has appointed you as leaders" (Acts 20:28 NLT).

First, notice that Paul—who is speaking to elders in this passage—says "guard yourselves." Only after that does he say to guard God's people. The order seems to be intentional. First watch out for yourself and also watch out for the people. We must not forget that. Paul was on to something here. If I could offer you only one warning as it pertains to being a leader others will follow, it would simply be this—stay alert!

One of the most common weapons that Satan uses on spiritual leaders is compromise. Compromise is the acceptance of a standard that is lower than desirable and exposes you to danger. This is especially true with regard to comprising in sinful behavior. If we become lethargic, inattentive, or calloused, the enemy has the opportunity to quietly and gradually lead us down a destructive path. Compromising your character can extinguish your leadership torch. This danger necessitates the warning—WATCH OUT! We must stay alert and be mindful of (1) the condition of our heart and (2) the performance of our hands. These are the two ways to guard yourself, and in my experience, there's a major temptation and pitfall for each of these:

Selfish Ambition: A Compromise of the Heart

Selfish ambition will contaminate a leader's motive for doing just about anything. Leaders who are blinded by this are many times referred to as self-serving leaders because their primary focus is what they can get. They are concerned with their own needs, desires, and interest, and put themselves ahead of those they lead.

Don't be selfish; don't try to impress others. Be humble, thinking of others as better than yourselves. Don't look out only for your own interests, but take an interest in others, too.

PHILIPPIANS 2:3–4 NLT

In *Lead Like Jesus*, Ken Blanchard says, "Self-promotion (pride) and self-protection (fear) are the reigning motivations that dominate the leadership landscape. Many leaders act as if the sheep are there only for the benefit of the shepherd."[18] For example, King Saul had no intention of becoming a narcissistic, egotistical, and power-hungry dictator, but as some leaders do, once he had power and influence, he lost his leadership bearings. He was seduced to the dark side of leadership. He no longer thought twice about imposing his will on people or destroying anyone who stood in his way.

You probably have heard someone say, "Oh, that will never happen to me," only to find out later that it did in fact happen to them. Typically, it's not because of a premeditated action, it's usually because they just "fell asleep at the wheel."

Even the disciples of Jesus got caught up in selfish ambition, and it came at the most inopportune moment—their last meal with Jesus before he was crucified. How could this happen? Selfishness is at the core of the human condition and will consume us the moment we stop fighting it. If we take the stance, This will never happen to me so I don't need to guard against it, we set ourselves up to fail. We must stay alert, be mindful, and guard our hearts against selfish ambition. We cannot allow it to creep into our hearts.

Consistently pray that God will help you to love and care for his sheep with an authentic heart. Ask God to give you a burden for those you lead and serve. See the flock entrusted to you with the perspective Jesus has of them: He loved them so intensely that he was willing to die for them. Intentionally look for ways to serve those you lead, which will hold you in check and help you keep a pure heart.

Mediocrity: A Compromise of Skillful Hands

As a young man I developed a habit that would hamper and limit my potential in every aspect of my life. I relied on natural ability without putting in the work to improve those natural abilities. As a result, my actions accomplished less than what they could have. My mom and dad did their best to get me to apply myself and be more disciplined, but I would find a way to cut corners.

I played multiple sports in school and was blessed with a degree of athletic ability. But because I had not disciplined myself, I relied completely on my natural mental and physical ability. I did very little to further develop those skills. In fact, I would tend to do just enough to get by. For example, in order to play football on Friday night in high school (or Saturday in college), I was required to maintain a certain grade point average. So I would find out what my grade point average had to be to be eligible to be on the field for game day, and my goal was to do just enough to get by. My poor parents! I know this frustrated them immensely. And even with them pushing me to be my best, I was content to do just enough.

One experience I'll never forget was a watershed moment for me as a person and future pastor. It was a conversation with my academic adviser in college my freshman year. (My grades were not great, which was the reason for the meeting.) She pointed out the areas I was struggling in in a matter-of-fact way and then abruptly asked me what I wanted to do with my life.

I paused for a moment and responded, "I'm going to be a pastor."

Her reaction jolted me. She leaned back in her chair and laughed out loud.

I was shocked. She was laughing in my face as if I had just told her the funniest joke she had ever heard. This was my professor! Once she regained her composure she leaned forward on her desk and said, "You'll never make it ministry."

Rarely am I at a loss for words, but I had no idea how to respond. Who was she to say, "You'll never make it in ministry"? She knew very little about me. In fact, all she did know about me was the fact that I was struggling with my grades. But the truth was she saw a pattern of laziness from a guy who just said he was going to be a pastor. No, she didn't know much about me, but what she did know was that I was not applying myself. I had been frustrating my parents, teachers, coaches, and myself for years. Unfortunately, I'm sure I was frustrating God with this habit as well. I had developed a pattern of settling for "just enough." There is a word for this and it's mediocrity.

Mediocrity is an existence of just doing enough to get by. It's a willingness to accept an effort that is "barely adequate" when there was potential for so much more. This habit turned into a lifestyle, and I was on a trajectory toward failure.

During this time, God, in his loving kindness, took something important from me to get my attention. One night during the middle of this difficult season, I felt impressed by the Holy Spirit to be alone with the Lord. So I walked to an elementary school behind my college campus and sat on a swing. I could feel God's presence in that dark playground and began talking to God. As I did, God spoke these words to me from Colossians 3:23–24: "Work willingly at whatever you do, as though you were working for the Lord rather than for people. Remember that the Lord will give you an inheritance as your reward, and that the Master you are serving is Christ" (NLT). I felt conviction as tangible as someone standing on my shoulders. God made it very clear to me that I was to glorify him in all areas of my life—including academics.

That event became a defining moment in my life. However, it didn't end there. That was just the wakeup call. The process started to break an ingrained pattern; it also developed a new habit of working hard with diligence and determination to reach my full potential.

Mediocrity is not an innate condition that a person must live with. It's the result of a habitual self-satisfaction that is blindly unaware of the damaging limitations to one's potential. In other words, complacency breeds mediocrity, and mediocrity prevents us from realizing our full potential as it compromises our "skillful hands." A habit that will prevent you from being a leader others will follow.

So, dear brothers and sisters, work hard to prove that you really are among those God has called and chosen. Do these things, and you will never fall away.

(2 PETER 1:10 NLT)

We must be alert and not compromise our skillful hands through mediocrity. Whatever you do, wherever you are, do it with excellence. Do the very best you can with what you have. As Paul said to the Colossians: "Whatever you do or say, do it as a representative of the Lord Jesus, giving thanks through him to God the Father" (Col. 3:17 NLT).

Wouldn't it be great if the people you led said about you, "I will follow that leader anywhere!"

A proclamation of commitment like this is not offered to a title or a position. It's presented to a leader who has proven to authentically care for people and embodies a skill set that elicits confidence and courage. This is the mark of a servant leader, a leader whose influence will have an exponential impact on this world and on the one to come.

You can be that leader. The qualities of a servant leader can be learned and developed through obedience and sacrifice as you fulfill the calling God placed on your life. It's not easy, but then again, if it were easy, everyone would do it. I'll end this chapter with the words of Paul: "Therefore I, a prisoner for serving the Lord, beg you to lead a life worthy of your calling, for you have been called by God" (Eph. 4:1 NLT).

Visit www.childrensministryonpurpose.com to download the free discussion guide with reflection questions and activities for Chapter 9. These activities and questions will help you learn how to increase your longevity in ministry through re-invention, think through steps to follow a difficult leader, and learn how you can lead up.

CHAPTER 10

The Importance of Involving Parents

In this section about thinking personally, we must consider the personal nature of working with parents. The goal of this chapter is to both encourage and challenge you. First, I want to encourage you in what you are already doing to partner with parents, even if it seems small to some and doesn't fit one of the varied definitions or descriptions of family ministry.

Second, I want to challenge you to examine your children's ministry to look for incremental steps you can take to both help parents understand their spiritual responsibility and to resource them in their efforts to influence their child's spiritual formation.

Throughout this book, I have presented concepts and processes related to being purposeful in your children's ministry along with practical examples from Saddleback's children's ministry to guide and inspire your thinking. As we now consider being purposeful with parents, I would like to highlight an important point before going any farther.

The absence of the word "family" or "parents" in the Saddleback Kids mission statement is not an indicator of our commitment (or lack of commitment) to the biological family. Just as it is dangerous to assume that the presence of a word in a mission or vision statement means it is being implemented, it is just as dangerous to assume its absence is a sign of neglect.

Family Involvement Gone Awry

Involving parents does not always go over well with the parents, even if it's best for the kids. For example, years ago the children's ministry I led was offering a new discipleship opportunity for elementary students. In preparation for the launch of this new endeavor, I hosted a gathering for parents to share my vision and goals, answer any questions, and hopefully establish a solid partnership. Unfortunately, not many parents showed up, but the ones that did seemed interested and very pleased with the plan. The message I wanted them leaving with that night was this: "Our objective is to support you the parent." If I said it once I said it twenty times. While I wanted to see more parents there, the night was a success. I was feeling good about what happened, until a few weeks went by.

I received a phone call from a parent who had attended the recent gathering. I knew this mom and her family well, but I was a little surprised when she told me they were having a "terrible time" with their daughter. This was surprising because she always seemed extremely well behaved. The mom said her disrespect was out of control and asked if I would meet with her. I agreed and we set a date and time. When the time came, the mom and daughter came to my office. After an initial conversation, I excused the mom so McKinsey and I could have a heart-to-heart discussion. All it took was one question.

"McKinsey, what's going on?" I asked. This little nine-year-old told me that her mom was forcing her to participate in

221

gymnastics, even though she didn't want to. Okay, I thought. But still no reason for massive disrespect.

But then McKinsey goes on to tell me her schedule: She is in the gym with her coach by 5:45 a.m. before school, which means wake-up time is 5:00 a.m. Practice goes until 7:00, then back home to get ready for school, go to school, go to another practice after school, come home, do homework, and go to bed. That was her schedule!

In tears she said, "I hate gymnastics. I just want to go home after school and play with my friends."

After hearing this, I dismissed McKinsey without saying much of anything to her. I called the mom into my office. This is where the conversation got interesting . . . and heated. I asked the mom why she brought her daughter to me.

She responded, "You said you wanted to support us. She doesn't want to be involved in gymnastics, but it's for her good. So I need you to tell her she should just do it."

I told the mom she was doing her child a disservice by robbing her of her childhood.

As you can imagine, this didn't go over so well. I had indeed said, "I'm here to support you," but what she wanted was not the kind of support I was offering.

The Purpose of the Biological Family

God designed the biological family for more than just populating the earth and forming a social infrastructure. The biological family unit was designed to be—and remains so today—the most significant influence in a person's life. While the direct influence of a parent will change with time, the impact of the foundational and formative influence from a parent will remain throughout a person's life. Unfortunately, this tremendous influence is not always good and has caused much pain and difficulty for those who did not have positive parental experiences.

This was never the intent, but it results from sin entering the world through disobedience.

God's master plan for humanity is intended to be accomplished in the context of the biological family through marriage. Keep in mind the primary purpose of the family, which is spiritual formation. Above all things, parents are to nurture and lead their children toward a thriving relationship with the living God. In fact, the Great Commandment in the Old Testament was originally given in the context of family life. This is the part of the verse most people know: "Listen, O Israel! The Lord is our God, the Lord alone. And you must love the Lord your God with all your heart, all your soul, and all your strength" (Deut. 6:4–5 NLT). But read the very next two verses about family: "You must commit yourselves wholeheartedly to these commands that I am giving you today. Repeat them again and again to *your children*. Talk about them when you are at home and when you are on the road, when you are going to bed and when you are getting up" (Deut. 6:6–7 NLT, emphasis mine).

When Jesus was asked about the most important commandment from God, he cited Deuteronomy 6, affirming the chief goal over a thousand years later. What's vital to understand here is the role of the biological family in helping children live out the most important commandment and the end goal of life. Note the nuance: Repeating them to your children (Deut. 6:7). We must disciple our own children and we must equip parents to disciple their children. If we don't do this, we're missing a major aspect of

God's heart. I began here because it's important to start with the importance of the biological family so that we can understand the weight of what Jesus says about the family of God.

> Jesus replied, "'You must love the Lord your God with all your heart, all your soul, and all your mind.' This is the first and greatest commandment. A second is equally important: 'Love your neighbor as yourself.' The entire law and all the demands of the prophets are based on these two commandments."

MATTHEW 22:37–40 NLT

The Church Is God's Family

The church is the single, multiethnic family promised by the creator God to Abraham. It was brought into being through Israel's Messiah, Jesus; it was called to bring the transformative news of God's rescuing justice to the whole creation.

N. T. WRIGHT, *SIMPLY CHRISTIAN*

This will sound like an oversimplification, but the church is God's family (see Eph. 2:19; 1 Pet. 2:17). It is a family made up of families. Jesus himself was born and raised in the context of a physical family. But the biblical understanding of family extends beyond biology, and the purpose of family extends into a larger spiritual realm. That's what Jesus was getting at one day, when the people told him that his family had come to see him: "Jesus asked, 'Who is my mother? Who are my brothers?' Then he pointed to his disciples and said, 'Look, these are my mother and brothers. Anyone who does the will of my Father in heaven is my brother and sister and mother!'" (Matt. 12:48–50 NLT).

In this passage Jesus was not saying that the physical or biological family is unimportant or that it should be discounted or ignored. He's saying that the spiritual family is the most important connection in a person's life—because they are connected through the kingdom of God, which is not limited by biology or circumstance, but available to everyone! We did not choose our biological families in our physical birth, but we do choose to be a part of the larger spectrum of family when we are spiritually "born again" into God's family. Our spiritual family consists of people "from every nation and tribe and people and language" (Rev. 7:9 NLT). These people make up the family of God, the church.

But to all who believed him and accepted him, he gave the right to become children of God. They are reborn—not with a physical birth resulting from human passion or plan, but a birth that comes from God.

(JOHN 1:12–13 NLT)

Where Did It All Change?

To better understand the present circumstances and consider possibilities in the future, it's important to have a picture of the past. In this case, I'm talking about the history of how family has worked in the United States. There was a time when education, economic productivity, care for the elderly, and spiritual formation happened inside the context of the biological family. Then came the industrial revolution, which launched a different type of lifestyle. Eventually, this redefined how the biological family functioned: Dads began working far from home, and not long after that, many moms entered the workplace. Just like a boulder rolling down a hill gaining momentum with every turn, each advancement in technology led to another transition within the functionality of the family. Within a short time, long-distance communication, modern transportation, and digital technology made a big world seem small. Along with the great advances and conveniences that accompany technology came a dynamic that forever changed family dynamics—the increased pace of life. For example, the Internet reinvented the concept of connection, making it possible for us to have instant, constant, and global connection with anyone or anything. When the Internet was first introduced, it appeared that this new and virtually unlimited connection would provide unprecedented conveniences, opportunities for learning, and the ability to network with anyone on the planet. And while this is true of the Internet, it is also true that this unlimited connection has created pressure to work longer hours and maintain an unrealistic number of relationships.

This pressure increased the pace of life, and we have never looked back or slowed down, only sped up. The faster pace of life and globalization increased the demand for productivity, forcing coping mechanisms called compartmentalization and specialization. No longer was every aspect of life streamlined and primarily based on the biological family unit. Now our specialization mandated that we delegate some formative and care-giving responsibilities outside the biological family.

As a result of these changing realities, the church adapted its methods. The goal was to meet the needs of the family, and in some ways that has happened. I seriously doubt anyone in church leadership set out to replace the parents as the primary influence in a child's spiritual formation. It appears to me that they saw a need and made adaptations to their methodology in an effort to support the family more effectively. But was it the right move for the church to adjust to a specialized form of discipleship that segregated the family at church? That's a difficult question to answer.

We may each have different perspectives of the ideal church-family collaborative relationship, but I think it is important to consider several realities that will certainly have a bearing on how the biological and spiritual families work together in the future:

- The definition of "family" can no longer be assumed as biological families are more varied and diverse than a generation ago.
- We are fighting to preserve a biblical view of family and marriage.
- The connection to extended family members has been greatly limited due to economic pressures for families to "go where the work is," making spiritual influence from them more limited.
- Attention spans of children are getting shorter and shorter.[19]
- Parents feel an incredible amount of pressure to have their kids involved in multiple activities and programs, which often compete with church and home life.
- Kids feel pressure to constantly perform at a high level due to increased competition for scholarships and employment opportunities.

- Families are less committed to church attendance because of the busyness of life.

So what are we to do? Give in to busyness and self-centeredness? Of course not. We must be open and honest about the realities we face and continually work toward solutions that please God. The biological family and the spiritual family, the church, were created by God with the intent that the two would work strategically together. We cannot deliberately relegate the spiritual formation of our children to either the biological family or the church alone. It must be a partnership between both family and church.

A Partnership Between Families: The Church and Parents

As we discuss the partnership between the church and parents, remember that the goal is spiritual health. The greatest opportunity for success in leading kids toward spiritual health is a strategic partnership between the parents and the church. When I say partnership, I mean a relationship between individuals or groups that is characterized by mutual cooperation and responsibility, as when working together to achieve a goal. Partnership creates synergy, which is two or more things working together to create something that is bigger or greater than the sum of their individual efforts.

A person standing alone can be attacked and defeated, but two can stand back-to-back and conquer. Three are even better, for a triple-braided cord is not easily broken.

ECCLESIASTES 4:12 NLT

The partnership we're talking about is an alliance between God, the biological family, and the church. There are three parties at work. When the church and parents work together with God at the center of their efforts, they have synergy. This synergy carries with it a much greater potential for effective discipleship for kids. Parents have the biggest potential impact on a child, but trying to disciple their kids without any help or support will limit their effectiveness. Kids need multiple positive influences in their life. This is where balance comes in: The church and parents working together in a partnership with the objective of moving kids toward spiritual health.

Who Disciples the Kids—the Church or the Parents?

The passage above, Deuteronomy 6:5–9, which contains the commandment to love God with everything in the context of family life presents a clear view that parents are to be the primary disciple maker of their children. The church is the secondary disciple maker of children. In other words, the parents teach and model spiritual truth and disciplines for their children, and the church supports the parents.

A disciple maker is a teacher. It comes from ancient roots and simply means, "to teach." In the original context—Greco-Roman and Jewish cultures—the focus of teaching was on shaping the person's life, not just their mind. So a disciple maker helps to shape the character and life of a person, not just the information they have in their mind.

A purpose driven children's ministry partners with parents by providing materials and training to equip parents as they develop into their role as the primary disciple makers. There are a number of good curriculums available that will accomplish this. At Saddleback, we use a curriculum called "The Journey" that intentionally and strategically puts parents in the "driver's seat" of this discipleship process. This happens on a pathway we call Kids Small Groups that we discussed in chapter 6.

However, not every parent at Saddleback Church is prepared to accept their role as the primary disciple maker. We have parents who are new believers and are just now learning what it means to be a Christ follower. For parents who are new believers, the idea of being the primary spiritual influence of their children is intimidating. We have other parents who have been believers for a while, but for different reasons, they still struggle with the responsibility of being the primary disciple maker of their children. Many of these parents feel inadequate and have a looming sense of "failure" hanging over them anytime the subject is mentioned. In honest conversations with parents, while it's obvious that they love and desire what's best for their children, the concept of discipleship in the home seems daunting and confusing to many of them. We must "demystify" the concept of the parent being the primary spiritual influencer of their children by guiding our parents through teaching, encouragement, and offering simple steps that will help them grow into this role. This is why a purpose driven children's ministry addresses both sides of discipleship for children—providing opportunities for children to know and grow in Christ through weekend services and midweek discipleship, while also equipping parents to disciple their kids in the home. When the parents are doing the work at home, we as the church collaboratively support them with relevant discipleship materials and tools.

Your ministry context is unique. Your church is not like other churches, and just because a model works in one church doesn't mean it will work in yours. Consider various factors, like your church's culture, the strategy and structure of your ministry, your senior pastor's perspective of partnerships with parents, and your facilities.

These are just a sampling of the factors that contribute to your ministry context. There is no "one size fits all" approach to ministry or partnership with parents that will succeed in every ministry setting. This is where you as the leader of children's ministry need to determine what steps you should take and when those steps should be taken.

The Importance of Maintaining Perspective

The word *perspective* comes from a Latin root word meaning "look through." In essence, each person's perspective is the frame through which they see and interpret the world. You can ask ten people to look at the same painting and you will probably hear ten different interpretations and opinions. This is because we see and interpret situations, events, conversations—even ministry— through lenses that have been unconsciously defined by our individual belief systems.

Think about your perspective and how it differs from other adults in your life. Many things, such as experiences, culture, travel, education, faith, family, hobbies, and values shape our perspectives. Our perspective is our reality. We don't always see things as they truly are. This is important to acknowledge because each of our perspectives also shapes our point of view or standpoint on ministry. I've seen this most clearly through my experience with children's ministry leaders who were led to Christ through an evangelistic event. They will typically lean toward a ministry model that features or emphasizes evangelical events—simply because that's what they experienced firsthand. Another way this plays out is in our interpretation of Scripture. As we consider the family unit and parenting responsibilities described in the Old and New Testaments, it's very difficult to separate our own personal perspectives and preconceptions as we read the text.

If we are not mindful of our perspectives and the preconceptions that are derived from those perspectives, we can easily misinterpret the stories of family life in the Bible and how they should be applied to the era we are living in today.

We need to be mindful when we talk about family ministry and partnering with parents. The danger is always in the extremes. Just as the church can inadvertently create an obstacle for parents in fulfilling their role as primary influencer, it is also possible to create an obstacle for parents by alienating them or by not being empathetic to their unique situations.

- Yes, the parent should spend quality and quantity time with their kids. But we must be cautious and compassionate when communicating this to the dad whose job requires him to travel extensively.
- Yes, the parent should be leading the spiritual formation of their child in the home. But we must be loving when communicating this truth to the single mom who has to maintain three jobs just to pay the bills.
- Yes, we should provide resources to parents that equip them to fulfill their role as primary spiritual influencer. But we must be cautious not to discourage the mom

or dad who struggles with depression and feels like a complete loser every time the subject comes up.

- Yes, we should remind parents that the spiritual formation of their kids is the parents' responsibility, according to the Bible. But we must be understanding of the grandparent who suddenly finds themselves the primary caregiver because their daughter was killed by her husband who then took his own life, leaving two kids without a parent.

- Yes, we need to equip the parent to teach and model Christlike living in the home. But we must do so with grace as many parents have split custody due to divorce and constantly battle the tension created by an ex-spouse who does not support or even condone Christ-centered teaching or living.

These scenarios are not hypothetical. Every one of them is an actual experience connected to people in my church. Because each family's situation is different, it's important that we approach our partnership with parents with grace and understanding. If parents feel church leadership is insensitive to their situation or putting more pressure on them than they can handle, we could jeopardize the partnership. It is the responsibility of church leaders, however, to "shepherd the flock." So, in the case of ignorance, the responsibility falls on the shepherd to know better than the sheep.

A word of caution: Just as multiple models and methods for children's ministry exist, so do many approaches to partnering and definitions of "family ministry." With that in mind it's vital to remember that we as leaders in children's ministry don't waste time and energy criticizing others for implementing a ministry method, model, or style that is different from ours. It's also important to be mindful of our personal preferences and preconceptions of how a children's ministry should partner with parents. Otherwise, I might fall into the trap of defending my stance on the issue to the detriment of my growth as a spiritual leader. There are many good things to be learned both from those who subscribe to my ministry conviction and those who do not.

Partnership Is a Process

The partnership between parents and church is a process much like the discipleship process. It happens is stages and steps. People start the process from different points. The spiritual maturity of the parent will often, though not always, reflect their involvement with the child's spiritual formation. It's helpful to remember that parents cannot lead children past their own spiritual maturity.

The circles of commitment that I shared with you earlier in the book can also be used to show the strategic involvement of parents at different levels. It aligns with their own level of spiritual growth and development.

Strategic involvement does not restrict a parent's involvement or limit the partnership, it's simply a guide for developing the involvement opportunities and tools. For example, we offer our Crowd parents simple online "parent helps" in the form of a summary of what the kids are learning on the weekend accompanied by the same teaching videos the kids watched at the weekend service. We also provide simple questions for the parents to use as a conversation guide to talk about the teaching.

Parents who are identified as Congregation, Committed, Core, or Commissioned, are equipped for and included in the small group

discipleship pathway. The curriculum we use is designed to involve parents in each lesson as described in chapter 6. We have classes for parents at each age level, offering instruction and guidance on making the most of their involvement in this process.

It's vital that you allow your parents to grow into the role of the primary spiritual influencer without the guilt and shame we can inadvertently put on them for not doing this sooner. Two great disciple makers, Jesus and Paul, gave people only what they could handle at the time. As the people matured, they were exposed to higher levels of teaching and responsibility. One of the keywords for this book is "journey." Just as we lead the kids on their journey toward spiritual health, the parents are on their own journey as well.

Take Some Practical Steps

There are some practical steps your children's ministry can take to strengthen purposeful partnerships with parents. These steps are "doable" and don't require a complete reinvention of your ministry.

Step 1: Fine-Tune Your Communication Rhythm. Effective communication with parents is an easy way to strengthen partnerships and build trust. Poor communication can do just the opposite. Create appropriate and relevant channels of communication for your parents. Be careful not to insist on using a method of communication that is comfortable to you but not well received by the parents. Routinely follow up with parents about your communication to ensure you are being effective. Make sure their information is correct. Your message needs to be simple, visually acceptable, and concise.

Step 2: Share the Calendar. With crazy schedules, you must be intentional about the events you schedule. For example, be aware of the number and types of events we are putting in front of our families. Offer a combination of age-specific events ("drop-off events"), as well as intergenerational or all-inclusive events with parents and kids. Make sure the events you offer are not competing with other ministries in the church.

Step 3: Create Connection Points. One way you can purposefully partner with parents is to create connection points where you can introduce (or reinforce) the biblical role of parents as the primary spiritual influence in their child's life. Also, take time to demonstrate how the church partners with them in leading their child toward spiritual health. A connecting point is the perfect time to make parents aware of the spiritual formation objectives in the next stage of their child's discipleship process at church. This can also be an opportunity for parents to ask questions or give vital feedback to current programming.

One of the most fruitful connection points is a milestone. This is a significant event or stage in a child's development. We celebrate three natural milestones at Saddleback Church, and we use these as connecting points with our parents. Each of these is an opportunity to equip and encourage them as the primary spiritual influence in their child's life. The three milestones are child dedication, baptism, and communion.

Milestone 1: Child Dedication

Any parent desiring to dedicate their child to God publicly is required to attend a Parent Commitment and Child Dedication class. One of the crucial objectives of the class is to make sure the parent is a believer and fully aware of the commitment they are making. In this class we teach parents what child dedication is and is not. We help them understand their God-given responsibilities as the primary influencer of their child's spiritual formation. We share with them the mission, vision, and values of our children's ministry and our commitment to support them in each stage of their child's spiritual development. We also give them parenting resources.

The ceremony itself varies depending on which Saddleback campus you attend. Most of our campuses perform the dedication ceremony during a weekend service. Some of our larger campuses have their Dedication Ceremony on Saturday morning with all the friends, family members, small group members, and whoever wants to support them. We make it a big deal with food, photographers, decorations—the whole nine yards. We consistently receive positive feedback from not only the parents involved but also from extended family members and friends who are invited to be a part of the ceremony. During this event, we share the message that we are all God's masterpiece from Ephesians 2:10. For some of the guests our parents invite to the ceremony, it's the first time they have heard that their identity, their purpose, and their destiny is in God.

Milestone 2: Baptism

Similar to a Child Dedication, parents are required to attend a baptism class with their child before they receive baptism. In this class, we teach both the child and the parent what baptism is and is not. A member of our team has a personal conversation (or "interview") with each to make sure they understand, based on Scripture, the step they are taking. There are times that we discover a child has not made a decision to make Jesus the Lord of their life. In such cases, we give them the opportunity to do so at that time. In fact, we also extend the invitation for salvation to the parents. This has been an incredibly fruitful practice for us, because we often have the opportunity to lead the parents to Christ too.

Milestone 3: Communion

Like baptism, communion was instituted by Christ himself. While baptism is a one-time event, communion is to be practiced regularly by Christ followers. Communion is taught strategically within our small group discipleship pathway. We create a special event in conjunction with the small group discipleship schedule, where communion is taught and administered to the kids and their parents. This is a special time for both the child and the parent. For some of our parents, this is their first experience learning or participating in communion.

The Importance of Transitions

Another way to create connecting points with parents is through transitions. These aren't quite the same as milestones—and they're not celebrated in the same way—but it's another opportunity to measure and celebrate growth. For example, a transition is when a child is moving up to the next age bracket in the children's ministry. This is a good time to host a simple gathering to encourage parents, inform them of the strategy for the next developmental stage in the discipleship process, and let them know what they can expect in the next phase. This doesn't have to be a big ceremony, just a simple gathering. We do this at four transitional periods before high school:

- Nursery to pre-school
- Pre-school to younger elementary
- Younger elementary to older elementary
- Older elementary to middle school—The Big Bridge Event

Even though churches differ on their methodology of involving parents in the discipleship process, we can all agree that the most effective means of leading kids toward spiritual health is a partnership with the biological family and the church family. A partnership is a collaborative relationship that develops and strengthens over time. Any step you take, or process you implement, that contributes to the growth of this partnership with parents is something to celebrate.

Visit www.childrensministryonpurpose.com to download the free discussion guide with reflection questions and activities for Chapter 10. These activities and questions will help you think through the opportunities you currently use to connect with parents through your ministry. You'll consider new ways to effectively involve and partner with parents in your ministry, and examine some simple steps you can implement to encourage parents to take the next step in becoming the primary faith influencer in their child's life.

CHAPTER 11

The Necessity of Implementing Change

T hat's not going to happen."

These were the exact words spoken to me during a meeting in my first church where I was trying to introduce a change in how we approached Sunday school. The statement came from a board member who had a long history of deep-rooted involvement with Sunday school. He made it clear that he had no interest in change. To him, the very idea of change was ridiculous. Part of the reason for this obstinacy was because, in his eyes, I was a young, inexperienced, hardheaded leader who wanted to do things differently.

And he was right—I was all of those things.

But this board member wasn't defending the current model as relevant or effective, and he wasn't fighting the proposed idea. He was simply fighting the "idea" of change.

Unfortunately, this scenario is all too common in the local church. And because this mindset exists, some have accepted the idea that change can't happen in the local church. Initiating and implementing change is difficult and challenging and might even appear to be impossible, but it is possible. However, it must be approached wisely and purposefully.

As you have read through the previous chapters and given

thought to your children's ministry's strategy and structure, you may have come to the realization that there are areas of your ministry that must change. This realization may challenge you and give you a burst of inspiration and energy. For others, it can be incredibly scary. Either way, change is very personal and it should be treated in that way. I believe after reading this chapter, you will be more encouraged and feel more equipped to take a step of faith and begin the process of initiating and implementing the change you feel is necessary to increase the health of your children's ministry. We'll examine some common principles of effective change and a simple technique that has a proven track record for initiating change that can be implemented without having a degree in psychology.

Change Is Inevitable, But I Still Don't Like It

Just when I get comfortable using a certain computer program, some software engineer decides to change it just to make my life miserable. Right in the middle of writing this book, in fact, the makers of Microsoft Word—one that I have used for many years and know quite well—decided to change the program completely! By the time this book is published, there will probably be a newer version of the program, and the one I'm complaining about now will be a distant memory.

That one example is a good description of life itself. Life is all about change. It's actually ironic that we struggle so much with change when our entire life experience is fueled by change. Change is a natural process for our physical bodies, for technology, our lifestyles, and even our relationship with Jesus. The whole idea of being born again and developing as Jesus' disciples is based on change! The apostle Paul said this much in his day: "The Lord—who is the Spirit—makes us more and more like him as we are changed into his glorious image" (2 Cor. 3:18 NLT; see also 5:17).

> *For time and the world do not stand still. Change is the law of life. And those who look only to the past or to the present are certain to miss the future.*

JOHN F. KENNEDY

So is there anything in life that remains the same? Yes! The one thing that does not and cannot change is the Word of God. As I said before, in a purpose driven approach to children's ministry, the foundation is built on the Great Commandment and the Great Commission. These are God's Word, which never changes. But everything else can and will eventually change as culture and lifestyles change.

There will come a day when the great idea or program I am implementing today will no longer be effective in reaching its original objective. When that day comes, will I recognize the need for change? Will I be willing and prepared to let go of the old and embrace the new? These are challenging questions every leader must ask themselves if they desire to be effective in leading kids toward spiritual health in a world of constant and inevitable change.

Why do people not like change?

The reasons we dislike and resist change varies, depending on the people involved and the culture of the church. However, there are some commonalties to change resistance that you can find almost everywhere you go because of one primordial similarity—human nature. A big part of the human nature condition is the fact that most people don't like to be pushed; they like to be led from out front.

I compiled a list of the top reasons people don't like change. This list may be helpful for you as you process change:

- People don't like change because they like to be in control.
- People don't like change when they are not a part of the process.
- People don't like change because it takes them out of their comfort zone.
- People don't like change because we are creatures of habit.
- People don't like change if they don't understand why change needs to happen.
- People don't like change when they have a strong connection with "the old way."
- People don't like change when they are apathetic.
- People don't like change when they can't picture it.
- People don't like change if there is a lack of trust.
- People may have a lack of trust in the leader driving the change.
- People may have a lack of trust in the process.
- People may have a lack of trust in the overall objective for the change.
- And the number one reason people don't like change: People don't like change because of fear.

Whether it's the fear of the unknown, fear of failure, or fear of personal loss, the prospect of change will many times create a wave of fear in people that can prevent them from seeing the true benefits of the change.

Three Approaches to the Change Process

Your approach to leading the change process can be the difference between change actually happening in your church and change not happening. I am no expert on the change process, but I have walked this road a number of times.

My experiences in the arena of making changes range from great success all the way down to complete failure. One of the key factors in successfully initiating and implementing change is the approach of the leader introducing the idea of change. There are two techniques or approaches to initiating and implementing change that I have never seen work. I call them the politician and the bulldozer.

The Politician. The Politician's primary objective is to gain and maintain everyone's favor. They take a poll, ask everyone what they want, and try to please as many people as possible. This doesn't work because you will NEVER make everyone happy.

The Bulldozer. The second unsuccessful technique is the Bulldozer. This leader knows exactly what he or she wants and simply forces everyone to adopt their idea. If you challenge this leader or the idea, you will get rolled over. This approach doesn't work for obvious reasons. But one specific reason is this: you can't build trust, alignment, and love on a team where the leader runs over the team with no regard to their input, knowledge, or feelings.

The Guide. The technique that has successfully worked for me is what I call the Guide. This leader chooses to guide their children's ministry leaders through a process that opens their minds to a current reality that is missing the mark and in need of further exploration. The mind is much like a parachute—it doesn't work until it's open. As their minds are opened and made aware of the present circumstances, the Guide progressively walks the team through a discovery and development process that strategically involves the team and utilizes the strengths, experience, and talents of the group. And here is the best part, you can do this!

You've walked a pathway of discovery through the previous chapters in this book, and now you are prepared to lead others down the same path.

As your mind has been opened up to new possibilities, there is a good chance you have experienced a renewed sense of passion and vision for the great things God wants to do in your children's ministry. Pray and trust that those who serve with you will have the same experience as you share what God has been speaking to you through this process.

You cannot force someone to follow you down a hiking trail. You'll be dragging them if they don't want to follow you! With that in mind, instead of trying to convince or force the leaders of your church or ministry that change needs to happen and present a twenty-page plan detailing your every move, just lead them down the same path you just walked. Sound risky? Sure it does! But everything valuable in my life felt risky at some point. If you want to grab the fruit, you have to climb out on a limb.

Before we go any farther, I need to make something absolutely clear. A leader who is guiding a team through a change process already has a good idea of where the process is going. Remember, you as the guide are leading the team through a process of discovery that has already become real to you. You have seen the destination, and now you are taking the team there. The key here is discovery process. The team is discovering, just as you did, through a process, and that takes time. So constantly remind yourself to be patient.

My Story of Change

Earlier in this book, I told you that once I learned about the Purpose Driven paradigm, I knew I had to make some changes. If the church I was in at the time had been a Purpose Driven church, it would have been a cake walk, but it was not. So the obvious and glaring question was this: How was I, the children's pastor, going to implement a strategy in the children's ministry that was not being utilized by the whole church?

The leadership of my church was not interested in the Purpose Driven methodology. At best, our approach to ministry had a few similarities to Purpose Driven. The fact is, we were doing good things, but the good things were neither strategic nor intentionally structured, which is the essence of Purpose Driven. I had introduced change in my first church, but that was nothing compared to what I was looking to do now. The changes I made in my first church were little things, but now I was looking to make radical changes.

With a new excitement from reading *The Purpose Driven Church*, I closely examined my situation to see what could be done. While I did have influence in the children's ministry, the church's culture was deeply rooted in various ministries and programs. In church language, we call these sacred cows. I have read a number of books and articles about slaying sacred cows in the church, but in my experience, most sacred cows are never slain, you have to wait until they die of old age.

I was aware that our children's ministry could be much more effective, and the sense of urgency grew stronger as this awareness became a conviction—for me, it went from "this *could* be done" to "this *must* be done." But how?

In a seven-day week, our kids were given about five different and unique messages. Between Sunday school in first service and children's church during second service, there were a few different messages. Then there were elective programs on Sunday morning, and Sunday and Wednesday night programs. All together, these programs created five different messages, and they were not building on one another. Instead, they were actually competing with each other. As I looked at each of these programs, I could honestly say that each one was done well. We had put a lot of energy and resources into each one and it showed. None of these programs was bad and few if any showed signs of diminishing results. However, I was now painfully aware of a reality that could not be ignored. We had a lot of isolated programs all competing for resources and energy with no clear objective or strategic connection.

Sadly, few of these programs (if any) intentionally involved the parents in the process of spiritually influencing their kids. We did not have a clear mission statement, and we did not have team values to guide our decision-making process. We had no reliable way of truly knowing if our efforts, energy, and investment of resources were making a difference (other than parents not complaining and kids seeming to enjoy themselves).

Knowing all of this, I was still working with a strong conviction that something had to change. Even though change had not been easy in the past, and for that matter never will be easy, I had to find a way to at least introduce some level of change. I could no longer keep up the status quo. I didn't have a complete game plan, but my first step was to collect some data points from the kids. I began conducting "interviews" with the kids about what they liked, what they didn't like, what they would like to see happen, and so on. Then I started asking them what they remembered about the teaching from each of the programs. What I found was this: 95 percent of them remembered the last thing they heard, if anything at all.

Now, you might be thinking, "Well, clearly you did a poor job communicating or they would have remembered." Trust me, we went down that path and "amped up" the object lessons, created more elaborate dramas, and designed better support videos. I doubled the amount of time I put into preparing those lessons and programs. What was the result six months later? The same as before: The kids primarily remembered the last thing they were taught or experienced. It was clear that something was missing. And that something was an intentional discipleship process that strategically and developmentally led kids toward spiritual health.

My eyes were opened by interviewing the kids. I learned so much in that process that I decided to try the same thing with the volunteers. I started randomly asking them questions like, How effective do you feel our children's ministry is in teaching God's Word to the kids in our church? Do you believe the kids in your class are engaged? How effective are you in communicating God's Word to the kids?

My eyes were once again opened as I casually talked with volunteers. It was clear that most of the volunteers had a genuine desire to be effective in their ministry to children. I noticed that some were simply "doing their time" and nothing more, but I was thrilled to know that most of the volunteer team members I talked with were fully committed to making a difference in the lives of the kids they served. A surprising number of volunteers had concerns similar to mine. They felt as if their efforts were falling short. Many times I heard them say, "The kids just aren't engaged." But most of the volunteers could not articulate what needed to be done differently in our children's ministry. They just felt that something was missing.

It was time to act. But how was I going to make these changes when my church leadership wasn't on board?

My Next Step: All-Hands Meeting

I decided to call a meeting of all the key volunteers in each area of our children's ministry. The intent was to create an open dialogue to follow up on the questions I had been asking them individually. I made the meeting a "big deal." I brought in food, made the room look nice, and spent time honoring the volunteers.

Then the main event began—I asked the first of only three questions (or so I thought) to process the situation with the group: "In your opinion, why do we do children's ministry in this church?" I made sure they knew there was no "wrong" answer. I asked for their opinion, because everyone has one. Also, it's a great was to get the people in the room engaged in the conversation. But it was much more than an ice breaker. Almost everyone in the room had a response. As the leader of the children's ministry, it was fun and encouraging to see the passion welling up in the room around "why we do children's ministry."

The discussion was lively and engaging. The responses ranged from theological and theoretical to very personal and emotional. After each person had a chance to respond, I posed the next question: "What are the needs, struggles, or obstacles our kids face today?"

Like their response to the first question, it seemed that almost every volunteer in the room had something to say. Their responses were not based on the latest findings by a government agency or a research group, they simply talked about the hurts and obstacles of the kids in their life. It started out factual and quickly became personal and emotional.

After the discussion went on for a while, I asked my last prepared question: "Having discussed why we do children's ministry and identified some of the needs and struggles of our kids, let me ask you one more question: Are we succeeding?"

Unlike the responses to the previous questions, there was silence. No one responded. In that moment, they realized the need for change. I didn't have to talk them into it. They came to that conclusion on their own. After a long silence, one of the key volunteer leaders in the room answered, "I don't think we are. I think we are doing good things, but I don't think we are succeeding to the point that we could. What should we do?"

Now they were asking me questions.

It's very important that I make something clear: I did not "trick" them or manipulate them to see things my way. All I did was direct their thinking with a few empowering questions. They arrived at this conclusion without me pleading or demanding. This method of guiding people's thoughts with empowering and guiding questions was modeled and mastered by none other than Jesus. "Questions were one of his primary tools to get people to stop, think, and change their lives."[20] (e.g., Mark 8:27–29). As I said before, my intention was to ask only three questions. But then I asked a fourth and unplanned question.

"What if we could design a ministry strategy that did properly address these issues and was effective in connecting these kids to God? Would you be willing to help me put it in place and implement it?"

Without hesitation, they all gave a resounding "Yes!"

With the support and involvement of the key volunteers, we began evaluating each program and designing a more effective strategy in reaching our kids. When I went into that meeting with the key volunteers, I already had an idea of what needed to be done, but I didn't lay out any plan. I would do that in the next meeting. And once again, I used questions to guide us together, rather than just tell them the plan.

The Key to Creating Lasting Change

To create lasting change in someone, there must be a change in thinking. Let me remind you of a key verse from chapter 2 where we explored the concept of a discipleship process: "Don't copy the behavior and customs of this world, but let God *transform* you into a new person by *changing* the way you think. Then you will learn to know God's will for you, which is good and pleasing and perfect" (Romans 12:2 NLT, emphasis mine).

God transforms us by changing the way we think. We can see this inside-out approach in Jesus' teaching at the Sermon on the Mount (see Matt. 5–7). Dramatic change in behavior or actions begins with a change in thought. This is also the key to successfully introducing change to any group of people. Lasting change happens when the thinking of those involved changes. And the launch point for change in thinking is discovery.

Moments of discovery have been the catalyst for changing how we think about our world throughout human history. Exploration of new civilizations, people, and cultures changed the way we thought about and viewed the world around us. Once these discoveries were made, we simply could not think about our world in the same way again. As Oliver Wendell Holmes said,

"Man's mind, once stretched by a new idea, never regains its original dimensions."

I already shared the story of how Rick's book *The Purpose Driven Church* changed the way I approached ministry in the local church. Before reading the book, I had certain assumptions and perspectives about what I thought was effective in ministry and had developed a particular set of patterns around that thinking. Once I **discovered** the biblical and intentional approach Rick presented in the book, my mind was opened up to a new way of thinking. This change **disrupted** the assumptions and patterns I had developed over the years.

This change eventually led to the **development** of a new pattern of ministry. This process caused such an impactful change in my thinking about ministry that I would never think about ministry the same way again. Here's a snapshot of the new pattern we developed:

Discovery → Disruption → Development

Some discoveries are instantly impactful, while others simply uncover another clue that keeps you on the right path. Not all discoveries are equal in their significance or impact, but every discovery is significant on some level because it disrupts old patterns of thinking and paves the way for lasting change.

A Purposeful Approach to Guiding Your Team through a Change Process

At the beginning of the chapter, I said change is possible, but it must be approached wisely and purposefully. You may have a deep passion for leading kids toward spiritual health and you may have a great plan in mind to make it happen, but you must be intentional and strategic in your approach to initiating change or your plan may never become a reality.

Here are some steps you can incorporate as you prepare to guide your team through the change process. What I'm describing is how to prepare your heart and mind before leading change. Before leading (or even introducing) change, talk to God about it. What is he saying to you about your specific situation? Ask yourself what is driving the change? Check your heart and motives before moving forward. Once you've gained clarity on those two questions, then proceed.

Knowing When to Change. There are appropriate times to introduce change and times when change may not be best in the overall rhythm of your children's ministry. One of the books that greatly influenced how I approach change is called *Leading Strategic Change*. Authors J. Stewart Black and Hal B. Gregersen identify three tactics to timing change:

Anticipatory Change: Anticipatory change is looking ahead and anticipating the need for potential change based on what you are currently seeing. The challenge with anticipatory change is that you may be the only one who recognizes the need for change. At this stage, the program or process in question may be good enough, but you can see the expiration date for this program.

Reactive Change: Reactive change is recognizing obvious signs and signals that change is necessary. Change at this stage is much easier and more common than at the anticipatory level. It does, however, come with a cost. At this stage you probably have lost some momentum with the program in question.

Crisis Change: Crisis change is the stage in the life cycle of a program where the need for change is painfully obvious. There is very little vision casting needed at this stage as most people connected to the program are probably asking for a change. Change at this stage is certainly less difficult than at the previous two stages, but it comes at a greater cost.[21]

Below is a graph of the difficulty and costs of change based on three types of change:

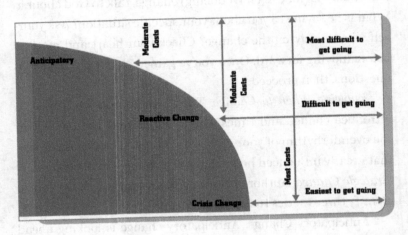

This picture illustrates the most optimal time to change a program or event. Every program or event has a peak. The peak represents the best years of a program. But as you can see, once something hits the peak, it begins a decline. Sometimes this decline is a fast decent and sometimes it is slower. Once a program peaks, it's natural for decline to begin. If possible, you want to introduce some type of change, maybe a slight change or maybe a complete change, while the decline is still closer to the top of the bell curve—ideally, somewhere between the anticipatory level and the reactive level. If the program declines all the way to the bottom, you'll have less of a challenge introducing the need for change, but you will have greater loss in resources,

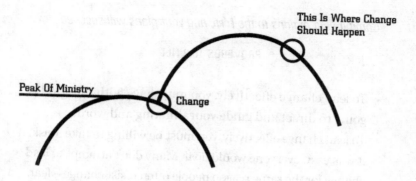

Peak Of Ministry

Change

This Is Where Change
Should Happen

momentum, and perception. The key is to start a new curve at the right time.

The Process. In order to really bring change home, you'll need to guide your leaders on the same journey of discovery that you experienced. Ask questions to help them discover the change for themselves. As I made clear in my story earlier in this chapter, asking intentional questions led my team to discover that we needed to make a change, and then together we identified what that change would be.

A Few Things to Have in Mind As You Lead the Change Process

There is so much to be said of change and the different aspects of the change process. Much has been written on the topic by people who know much more about the dynamics of change than I do. My intent was to share my experience leading the change process and spark some ideas in your mind of how you can confidently lead this process with your team. As I close the chapter, I would like to leave you with a few thoughts about change that could be helpful as you lead the change process:

Commit your actions to the LORD, and your plans will succeed.

(PROVERBS 16:3 NLT)

- To lead change effectively, you must have faith that God is going to direct and guide your thinking and words.
- To lead change effectively, you must be willing to take a risk. If it was easy, everyone would do it. Many don't attempt to lead change for the same reason people often resist change—fear.
- To lead change, you must not allow fear to prevent you from taking risks.
- To lead change effectively, you must be patiently persistent. This process will not happen overnight; it will take time.
- To lead change effectively, you must trust the process. Like a farmer who plants a seed and trusts the ground to do its work even though he can't see the progress, so too you must trust the process even if you can't see how it's developing.
- To lead change effectively, you must be adaptable. There is a really good chance that things will not go exactly as planned, and when it does, go with the flow as you follow the Lord.
- To lead change effectively, you must carefully choose the language that best fits your church's culture. If you feel using the language "purpose driven" might slow the process or create an obstacle because of a preconceived idea, use different language that fits your culture.
- To lead change effectively you must respect the past while you point to a new future. Show how the programs that are changing were instrumental in bringing you to where you are today, but what got you to where you are today will not get you to where you want to go tomorrow.

- To lead change effectively, be prepared to balance the old while you bring in the new. As you implement new strategies and structures into your ministry, you will probably need to maintain some of the previous model of practices while you usher in the new.
- To lead change effectively, you must create a sense of urgency. If your team feels "things are just fine the way they are," you will have a very difficult time leading them through the next steps in the discovery process.
- To lead change effectively, you need to "show" your team, not just "tell" them. The visual of the Map has been an effective tool in showing team members where we are leading the kids and how we are going to get them there.
- To lead change effectively, you must be prepared to leave some volunteers behind. The bottom line is that no matter how compelling the vision, some people simply will not want to make the journey with you. Whatever you do, do not talk them into remaining on the team.
- To lead change effectively, make small moves. Small moves consistently over time will get you where you want to go.
- To lead change effectively, create and celebrate short-term wins. Intentionally find small wins that your team can celebrate together.
- To lead change effectively, frame new programs, strategies, or structures as an experiment. Just using the word "experiment" softens the resistant team member's attitude because it doesn't have a sense of finality to it.
- To lead change effectively, you must be strategic with who you involve at each stage of the process (senior pastor, children's staff, key volunteers, and children's ministry

volunteers). It's probably not wise to include the entire volunteer team in the initial phase of the change process. You begin with the top level of leadership and incrementally add others as you go.

No, dear brothers and sisters, I have not achieved it, but I focus on this one thing: Forgetting the past and looking forward to what lies ahead, I press on to reach the end of the race and receive the heavenly prize for which God, through Christ Jesus, is calling us.

PHILIPPIANS 3:13–14 NLT

If you're reading this and you're not the decision maker for your children's ministry at your church, you can still follow this process of change. Simply invite your children's ministry pastor or director to go on a process of discovery with you, asking guiding questions, gaining clarity, and bringing solutions to the table. Leading change is not about manipulating others to do things your way. It's a process of discovery that opens a person's mind to new possibilities. This discovery will prayerfully disrupt old patterns of thinking and methodology and eventually lead to the development of a more effective approach of leading kids toward spiritual health.

The change process begins with you. If you can see the destination, you can lead others on the same pathway of discovery.

Visit www.childrensministryonpurpose.com to download the free discussion guide with reflection questions and activities for Chapter 11. These activities and questions are helpful in guiding your ministry team through the change process.

CHAPTER 12

Why Do You Exist in Ministry?

*But my life is worth nothing to me unless I use it for
finishing the work assigned me by the Lord Jesus—
the work of telling others the Good News about the
wonderful grace of God.*

ACTS 20:24 NLT

The apostle Paul was one of the most interesting and influential men in history. This highly educated and brilliantly insightful charismatic leader held fierce convictions, but those convictions were misguided early in his life. After he had a personal encounter with Jesus, his life was transformed, and the very talents he initially used to destroy the church were being used to build the church. Blind ambition was converted to crystal-clear purpose as Paul developed deep devotion to his Savior and to the calling placed on his life. Through many experiences, Jesus shaped Paul into an unforgettable person. Paul became one of the most significant influences in Christianity. In conjunction with the divine call on his life and the power of the Holy Spirit, the reason Paul was so effective was because he had a very clear purpose. Paul revealed his purpose for ministry in Acts 20:24 when he said, "But my life is worth nothing to me unless I use it for finishing the work assigned me by the Lord Jesus—the work of telling others the Good News about the wonderful grace of God" (NLT).

From this verse, we can detect Paul's clear purpose for ministry and the passion that ensued from his calling. Paul's ministry was met with many obstacles. Things were not easy for him, but he was able to endure because he had a clear sense of purpose. For Paul, self-preservation and personal gain were not factors as he considered the urgency and significance of the task given to him by God. Nothing mattered more to him than the completion of his mission. The drive and commitment we see in Paul's life existed because he understood why he was in ministry.

> *What matters is not the duration of your life, what matters is the donation of your life. What matters in life is not how long you live, it's how you live.*

RICK WARREN

The pivotal moment of understanding and embracing our purpose in ministry comes when we answer the question, "Why do I exist in ministry?" It is the same foundational question we asked in chapter 3 as we began the process of discovering more effective ways of leading kids toward spiritual health. Now, however, we are personalizing this catalytic question as we look to discover why we do what we do.

Ministry, whether paid or volunteer, is not for the faint of heart. There is no glitz, glamour, or glory about it. There is no promise of ease or of perks like in the corporate world. Sadly, most of the people I knew in ministry when I first started are no longer serving in ministry. While the circumstances varied, there are some common denominators that can't be ignored. Ministry is full of great joys, but alongside those great joys are heartache, disappointment, disillusionment, and personal pain.

Let's go back to the key question of why? Paul's words in Acts were very personal when he said, "But my life is worth nothing to me unless I use it for finishing the work assigned me by the Lord Jesus." These words have pierced my soul over the years, and they have been a source of inspiration. Now, I have never been physically beaten because I am a Christ follower, but I have experienced the disillusionment of watching senior leaders in ministry intentionally mislead people. I've seen Christian leaders lie; I've experienced the heartbreak of betrayal by those I thought were trusted friends; and I have experienced the disappointment of feeling that no one cares about what I do and no one would care if I didn't do it. But, even in all of that, the words of Paul resonate in my heart and mind—my life is worth nothing unless I do the very thing God put me on this earth to do.

That is the why question that you must settle in your heart and mind. Why do you exist in ministry? Once you work through the process of answering that question, the heartache, the difficulties, the disappointments—all of it will begin to fade, and you'll be overwhelmed with a sense of excitement and joy to fulfill the specific and unique task that God has given you. Knowing and understanding why you exist in ministry gives you a clear sense of purpose that provides the perseverance, passion, and perspective necessary to overcome the difficulties of ministry and thrive instead of merely survive. I want to dig deeper into each of these elements of purpose, starting with perseverance.

The words of the apostle Paul in 1 Corinthians 15:58 (NLT) give us a basis for knowing why we exist in ministry: "So, my dear brothers and sisters, be strong and immovable. Always work enthusiastically for the Lord, for you know that nothing you do for the Lord is ever useless."

Knowing Why Leads to Perseverance

I see a great example of perseverance whenever I look at the way buildings are constructed in Southern California where I live. In this area, earthquakes are common, even though most of the time they are so small we barely feel them. Experts forecast potentially large and destructive earthquakes in the immediate future, so structural engineers and architects have designed many buildings in the greater Los Angeles area to withstand the seismic activity associated with an earthquake. As I understand it, the buildings are constructed with incredibly strong foundations and are designed to bend but not break with the earthquake. These structures are not totally immune to the effects of a large earthquake, but advancements in engineering and design have made these building stronger and more immovable than ever.

When you have clearly answered the "why do I exist in ministry" question, you lay a firm foundation for your ministry and are better prepared for the seismic activity that comes with ministry. We have a word for the seismic activity we experience in ministry—storms. This foundation of purpose keeps you anchored and enables you to persevere when the storms come blowing through. Storms may burst onto the scene in a variety of forms, such as frustration, fatigue, fear, even doubt. While we all experience different types of storms in life and ministry, there are three storms that seem to be quite common for those of us in children's ministry that I would like to highlight.

Discouragement

I wish I could tell you there is only joy in ministry. But you and I both know that discouragement is bound to come. Throughout my years of ministry, I have experienced many moments in which my self-confidence, eagerness, or enjoyment of ministry were absolutely crushed by discouragement.

One form of discouragement is criticism, which is often far more present than encouragement. And it really hurts when positive feedback comes with negative words too. Another common form of discouragement is consistently working hard with little to show for your efforts. We plow the land, plant seeds, nurture the soil, and expect a big harvest. After a while this wears on you and the zeal that fueled your commitment begins to give way to discouragement.

Even in the process of writing this book, I have stared discouragement right in the eye. I have experienced greater inadequacies writing this book than during any other period of my life. Several times I have said, "I quit, I can't do this." But each time I go back to why I exist in ministry. While the discouragement doesn't disappear forever, I'm able to press on and keep moving forward. When I know why I exist in ministry, I am reminded that God chose me and empowered me to fulfill a unique purpose. I can serve with joy in the midst of discouraging circumstances, knowing that God is with me.

Bitterness

When I was in the interview process with Saddleback Church, I was asked a question by one of the executive leaders that I don't remember anyone ever asking me before. He said, "Steve, who is your hero?" Without hesitation I responded, "My dad." One of the reasons my dad has always been my hero is because he taught me how to weather the temptations of bitterness.

One particular occasion revealed my dad's heart about

forgiveness over bitterness. It was one of the unfortunate occasions in local church ministry. A church leader intentionally misrepresented my dad to some key decision makers at the church to hurt his reputation. This pastor was jealous, which led to actions unfitting of a spiritual leader. My dad could have been angry and taken this guy down and set the record straight. But my dad knew that setting the record straight would damage the local church.

My dad said to me, "It's not worth it to clear my name and hurt the church in the process." I was old enough to know what was going on. As a teenage boy, it was difficult to see this kind of behavior from spiritual leaders in a church. It was simply unbelievable. I was angry and wanted to address the matter face-to-face—with no intention of doing so in a loving manner.

My dad was wise enough to understand something I did not, namely that bitterness will kill you. Yes, what had happened to my dad was wrong and unfair, but unfair things happen all the time—even in the church world.

When we harbor unforgiveness, hurt, abuse, rejection, or pain, we give bitterness the opportunity to develop roots in our hearts. The roots of bitterness that grow beneath the surface slowly establish a strong and diabolical grip on every aspect of our life. It produces an infectious spiritual disease that continues to spread throughout your inner being and eventually damages not only you but others.

Look after each other so that none of you fails to receive the grace of God. Watch out that no poisonous root of bitterness grows up to trouble you, corrupting many.

HEBREWS 12:15 NLT

Then my dad went a step further and did something totally unexpected. He asked me to go with him to drop off a letter. As we approached the large mailbox receptacle at the post office, my dad explained the letter he was holding in his hand. He told me it was a letter to the individual who was intentionally causing pain in his life. The letter was an apology from my dad to the one fabricating the lies, asking him to forgive my dad for the bitterness and anger my dad was harboring in his heart. I remember thinking, "Wait, this is backward. You shouldn't be apologizing to him, he should be apologizing to you and taking responsibility for his wrongful actions."

As my dad dropped the letter into the mailbox, he said, "Steve, bitterness will kill you. It doesn't matter who is to blame or who is in the wrong. What matters is that you guard your heart from bitterness. If you don't, the enemy has an open door to destroy you and prevent you from doing what God has called you to do."

As he released the letter, the opportunity for resentment and bitterness went with it. He said, "It feels like a heavy weight has been lifted off my shoulders." I watched him rejoice as we drove home, free of all bitterness. Knowing why you exist in ministry empowers you to respond to hurt, pain, or rejection with intentional obedience and not react with vengeful emotions.

Drift

Have you ever been in a canoe or small boat on a lake? If you have, then you will clearly understand drift. The word *drift* means to be carried slowly by a current of air or water. It just takes a small amount of wind to push a boat off course.

Just like drifting on the water, drift can happen in people's lives and vocations as well. Peter Greer and Chris Horst state in their book *Mission Drift*, "But as organizations are made up of individuals foiled by pride and sin and allured by success, we conclude that this unspoken crisis isn't an organizational problem. It's a human one."[22] The principle of drift happens in ministry when we allow ourselves to forget why we are in ministry in the first place. We start off strong, but the winds and waves of life continually beat against us. If we are not strong and immovable, we will slowly be carried far away from that point at which we entered ministry. How does one know if they are drifting? Ask yourself these questions:

- Have you lost your joy for children's ministry?
- Do you find yourself constantly speaking negatively about your church?
- Do you have a take it or leave it attitude about your ministry?

Again, please understand that we have all been there. I have caught myself many times in a state of drift. Drift is gradual and usually quiet—but very destructive.

Consider the drift that happened to a well-known university in America. A simple look at their mission statement reveals how far they have wandered. Their purpose was "to be plainly instructed and considered well that the main end of your life and studies is to know God and Jesus Christ." This was the mission statement for Harvard University, which was established in 1636. At the start, this university employed exclusively Christian professors and rooted all of its policies and practices on biblical principles. Today it's regarded as a godless institution. They clearly drifted from their original purpose.

There are examples of mission drift in the church, in governments, in corporations, and in educational institutions, but it always starts with individuals. We all must navigate the currents of life that are in constant motion, attempting to toss us about here and there. Knowing why you exist in ministry keeps you aware of your current state of mind and keeps you on course toward the calling and purpose God has destined for you.

The Storms Make You Strong and Immovable

No one in ministry is immune to these obstacles and, if given a choice, I would love to go about my life and ministry without them. However, just as your life has purpose, so do obstacles we face—to keep you from your goal.

An experiment done in the early 1980s reveals how storms can make something strong. It occurred in a biodome as an exercise to create the perfect living environment for human beings, plants, and animal life. It was a biodome because a glass dome was built and an artificial, controlled environment was created with purified air and water and filtered light. All of this was supposed to create the perfect growing conditions for plants and wildlife and humans. There was one exception, however, to this perfect environment.

The trees within the biodome would grow and grow, eventually getting to a certain height, but would then topple over. It baffled scientists for quite some time until they realized one important natural element about nature—wind! You see, trees need wind to blow against them for their root systems to grow deeper into the soil. Without wind, roots will not grow deeper. And without deep roots, trees cannot grow to their full potential. The tension placed on the trees by the wind actually helps to develop the strength of the trees. Romans 5:3–4 makes it clear that difficulties and trials may be painful when the wind is blowing against us, but it makes us stronger: "We can rejoice, too, when we run into problems and trials, for we know that they help us develop endurance. And endurance develops strength of character, and character strengthens our confident hope of salvation" (NLT).

Viktor Frankl in *Man's Search for Meaning* writes:

> What man actually needs is not a tensionless state, but rather the striving and struggling for some goal worthy of him. What he needs is not the discharge of tension at any cost, but the call of potential meaning waiting to be fulfilled by him.[23]

When you know the answer to the question, "Why do I exist in ministry?" these challenges will not push you over. Instead, they will push our roots down just a bit farther and make us strong and immovable.

Knowing Why Leads to Passion

There is another word for this type of enthusiasm, and it's called passion. Without passion, you will not only find it impossible to reach your full potential in ministry, you will not last long in ministry. But with passion, you can experience the motivation, the energy, the engagement, and the drive necessary to accomplish anything God lays on your heart. In 1967 Dr. Martin Luther King Jr. delivered a speech in which he said, "If a man is called to be a street sweeper, he should sweep streets even as Michelangelo painted, or Beethoven composed music, or Shakespeare wrote poetry. He should sweep streets so well that all the hosts of heaven and earth will pause to say, here lived a great street sweeper who did his job well." He's saying whatever you do, do it with passion.

Passion is a red hot flame that can light a dark room. It's not just a feeling of optimism, it's a burning sensation deep within your soul that fuels your body and mind. Authentic passion cannot be ignored or hidden; it must be acted on. Passion drives us forward through hardship and pain, stimulates our thinking, and brings out the best in who we are. German philosopher Georg Hegel once said, "Nothing great in the world has been accomplished without passion."

Passion is that game-changing element that pushes us further and harder and keeps us energized and engaged, regardless of the extenuating circumstances. When we know why we exist in ministry, that sense of passion rises up within us. Romans 12:11 says, "Never be lazy, but work hard and serve the Lord enthusiastically" (NLT). There is that word again—enthusiastically. You see, when you know why you exist in ministry, you have purpose, and purpose always produces passion.

In my years of ministry, there have been numerous times when a leader or volunteer has come to me and expressed that they have lost their passion. They tell me that they no longer want to volunteer, that they have lost their desire to do the job, and that they are not sure they want to invest more time into ministry. My first question to them is always focused on their sense of purpose. I ask them, "Why are you doing what you are doing?" because I always go back to that primary question.

The Great Enemy of Passion

Knowing your purpose fuels your passion. There is a word in Scripture called *fervor*. In James 5:16, it talks about the fervent prayer of a righteous man, which is powerful and effective. The word *fervor* means boiling hot. For something to be hot, there must be a source of heat. For example, if you have a pot of boiling water on the stove and remove the water from the stove, the source of heat, the water will eventually return to room temperature. To remain boiling, it must remain on the heat source. This is what happens when you lose touch with your source of purpose. Your passion begins to wane, just as boiling water removed from the stove returns to room temperature. You become lukewarm. There is another word for lukewarm—apathy.

Apathy is the great enemy of passion. Apathy is the result of lost fervor, and this loss becomes obvious when you have a "eh, whatever" attitude. You are no longer hot and no longer cold, simply lukewarm. The descent from passion to apathy is not reflective of a character flaw, nor does it mean the person struggling with apathy is doomed. As I said before, it's something with which we all struggle. It's not a question of whether it will, but when it happens. At that point, how will you respond?

> *"I know all the things you do, that you are neither hot nor cold. I wish that you were one or the other!"*
>
> REVELATION 3:15 NLT

As I was preparing for one of our annual ministry themes, I asked God to give me a word of encouragement and inspiration for our children's ministry staff and volunteers to remind them of their purpose and calling. He led me to develop what I ended up calling the Commissioning Letter. After distributing the Commissioning Letter, I recommended to our team of staff and volunteers that they place it somewhere visible and read it often. My goal was to encourage and inspire them, but as the ministry season progressed, it became clear that God was speaking directly to me. While they benefited from it, I benefited from writing it even more than they did reading it. Here is the Commission Letter:

> I acknowledge and accept the commission given to me by my Lord and Savior Jesus Christ.
>
> Understanding that the enemy is deceptive and determined, I remain confident, courageous, and committed to the mission and accept my specific role and responsibilities to the mission.
>
> I will allow no enemy, seen or unseen, to distract, diminish, or destroy the destiny that awaits me. Though I may feel fear, I will not be controlled by fear. But with faith, I will move forward, trusting my God, and will embrace the overwhelming victory that has been promised by the One who commissioned me.

My commissioning letter is framed in my office, just feet away from my desk. There have been many moments when the demands, frustrations, or fatigue that come with ministry in the local church got the best of me, and I stood in front of that framed letter. Repeating those words out loud has brought me to the point of tears. I'm thankful that God gives us moments like this that emphasize our purpose, reignite our passion, and remind us for whom we are working. As Paul said, "Whatever you do, work at it with all your heart, as working for the Lord, not for human masters, since you know that you will receive an inheritance from the Lord as a reward. It is the Lord Christ you are serving" (Col. 3:23–24).

At the end of the day, we work for an audience of one. Do everything as if you were doing it for the Lord. If you find yourself feeling a little lukewarm, or if you are finding it difficult to overcome apathetic feelings, remember you are not alone and God has already given you what you need to reignite the flame of passion. A new gift or a new endowment of God's power is not really necessary. You just need to fan the embers inside your heart and create the conditions suitable for your passion to burn again.

This is why I remind you to fan into flames the spiritual gift God gave you when I laid my hands on you.

2 TIMOTHY 1:6 NLT

Knowing Why Gives You Perspective

How is it that two people can see the same movie, read the same book, look at the same piece of art, or witness the same event, but have completely different interpretations of what they saw or read? It's because of perspective. Perspective is the lens through which you see and interpret the world around you. Your perspective is your reality. A person's perspective, or the way they see things, is shaped by many factors, such as family, education, life experiences, travel. Whether we are consciously aware of it or not, our perspective has tremendous influence on our attitude and approach to life and ministry.

This is significant because so much of what we do in children's ministry is behind the scenes and can go unnoticed. There have been many times when I felt like my tireless efforts were overlooked or ignored, and it caused me to wonder if those tasks were a waste of time. The apostle Paul's words reframe my perspective and remind me that nothing I do for the Lord is ever useless. No matter how small, menial, or unnoticed a task may seem, if it's for the kingdom, then it's worth it. Sometimes we forget that the little things in ministry are just as necessary as the big, noticeable accomplishments. Everything we do in children's ministry, big or small, noticed or unnoticed, contributes to the big picture.

It's like working on a jigsaw puzzle. You have nearly completed the puzzle and only have one piece left, but you can't find that last piece! You can feel a sense of accomplishment because most of the puzzle is complete, but every time you look at the puzzle, your eyes are drawn to where that missing piece is supposed to fit. The puzzle is incomplete.

We have many tasks to accomplish in ministry, and we must know that it all contributes to the big picture. Each piece is important, each task or assignment is important, even when we don't feel it makes a difference. Time is our most precious commodity. It's the one thing we cannot reproduce or get back. That's why we want our efforts to actually matter. We want to know that our investment of time and energy contributed in some way.

In John 9:4 Jesus says, "We must quickly carry out the tasks assigned us by the one who sent us. The night is coming, and then no one can work" (NLT). There is a clock and it's ticking. There will come a day when our time is done. We must work enthusiastically for the Lord and be conscious of how we use our time. But in doing so we must embrace the truth of this verse. Everything we do for the Lord and his kingdom is worth the time, the effort, and the energy, even if others don't notice or we don't receive credit for our work.

My contribution to the kingdom of God is one very small piece to a very large puzzle. But even though I'm a very small piece to the puzzle, my piece is still important. It may not be flashy, it may not be on billboards around town, it may not be talked about on TV talk shows, but my small piece to the puzzle matters. And each and every action we take that is connected to the Lord's work matters. This truth alone is a game changer. It reminds me that I have a purpose and my purpose, no matter how its interpreted by others, matters to the kingdom. Mihaly Csikszentmihalyi, the author of the book *Flow*, wrote, "One cannot lead a life that is truly excellent without feeling that one belongs to something greater and more permanent than oneself."[24] What a great privilege and joy to know that what we do is a part of something so much bigger and more significant than our own lives. Nothing we do for the kingdom is useless . . . it all matters.

Do You Know Why You Exist in Children's Ministry?

Knowing your purpose by answering the "Why do I exist in ministry" question will make you strong and immovable, it will increase your passion, it will give you confidence that what you do matters. This will sustain you as you produce lasting fruit for God's kingdom.

Knowing why you exist in ministry will give you the foundation you need to navigate the feelings of fear, doubt, discouragement, and disillusionment, without being controlled by those feelings. Our purpose in ministry will push us through the tough moments and into a realm of joy and satisfaction as we do kingdom work.

If I asked you to articulate in a sentence why you exist in children's ministry, could you do it? If you had asked me that question just two years ago, I would have answered no. I have always been sure of my calling to ministry, because it was definite and clear. In fact, I began serving in children's ministry in the third grade and have been active in local church ministry ever since. However, I had never articulated, in writing, my purpose in ministry until I wrote my personal mission statement.

Since developing my personal mission statement, I have asked children's ministry leaders all over the world to articulate why they are in ministry and, interestingly enough, 99 percent of the time when I ask someone that question they have no response. I want to invite you to do a little exercise that could literally be the difference between you staying in ministry and quitting. It begins by answering this question—why do you do what you do?

This process has been incredibly beneficial for me personally. Something special, and I might add spiritual, happened as I wrestled with this statement. Since writing my personal mission statement, I have a renewed passion, vision, and commitment to children's ministry.

You may be tempted to shortcut this process or skip over it all together. Believe me, I'm the impatient person who would do just that, so I know how you feel. However, having walked through this myself, I can honestly say it's worth every minute.

As we draw near to the conclusion of this book, I would ask that you read the last few pages of the next and final chapter carefully and prayerfully and be prepared for God to spark a new sense of urgency within your heart.

Visit www.childrensministryonpurpose.com to download the free discussion guide with reflection questions and activities for Chapter 12. These activities and questions will help you to develop perseverance, passion, and perspective in your ministry. You'll also receive practical guidance in writing out your own personal mission statement.

Conclusion: One Generation Away

Imagine with me that you're sitting on the edge of your child's or grandchild's bed, sharing the beautiful Christmas story with them before they drift to sleep. As you finish emphasizing the wondrous love of God and his plan to redeem creation, the child, whom you love deeply, looks up at you and exclaims, "That's one of my favorite fairytales!" Immediately taken aback, you respond, "Well, you know that's not a fairytale, right? This actually happened. God sent his Son, Jesus, to this earth with a very special mission to save you and me from all the bad things in life, those things we call sin." The child looks up with all the seriousness he can muster in readying his honest response and says, "It's a good story, but we all know it isn't real."

How would we feel if the Christmas and Easter stories were reduced to nothing more than a cute childhood fairytale nestled alongside Aladdin's lamp, Cinderella's glass slipper, and the adventures of Elsa and Anna in *Frozen*? These are good stories with a strong, ethical component, but at the end of the day, they are entirely fictional tales. Does it unsettle you when you see God viewed in the same light as Santa Claus, Harry Potter, and Batman—fictitious characters who serve as the subjects of trendy stories with some moral guidance and encouragement thrown in for good measure?

What would happen if the next generation reduced the truth of God's Word to mere fiction? What if the next generation viewed the life of Jesus as mere mythology and the cross as nothing more than a cool tattoo? What if the next generation simply forgot about the one true God?

As you read this, you might be thinking, "That's impossible, Steve. There is no way that could realistically ever happen." Friend, the reality is that we are always just one generation away from the extinction of Christianity. I don't know what feeling that evokes within you, but it makes me feel sick to my stomach. The very thought of those I love being strategically and deceptively led down a path of destruction right under my nose literally makes me sick.

This sick feeling is what Bill Hybels brilliantly identifies as a "firestorm-of-frustration moment" in his book *Holy Discontent*. This internal firestorm is a defining moment in which our hearts are wrecked and broken, a moment that fuels a raging fire deep inside our souls. This raging fire drives us to a point in which we have seen and heard enough and demand that something be done about it. Hybels says, "Truth be told, the most inspired, motivated, and driven people I know are the ones who live their lives from the energy of their holy discontent."[25]

We Are Just One Generation Away

There is a story in the Old Testament that has created a holy discontent in my heart and fueled a passion and determination to make the most of every opportunity in my ministry to children and families.

This is not a positive story, though; instead it's one of failure on the part of God's people, just after they entered the Promised

Land. Here's a summary of how the people of God were just one generation away from totally forgetting God: "After that whole generation had been gathered to their ancestors, another generation grew up who knew neither the LORD nor what he had done for Israel" (Judges 2:10).

This passage represents the Israelites' failure to carry out their assignment given by God. In the wake of their failure, an entire generation grew up without knowing the one true God. In essence, they failed to obey God, and then God became irrelevant to them.

Why didn't the Israelites simply follow God? Maybe they were tired of fighting. Maybe they recognized an opportunity for economic expansion. Maybe they had lost their unifying purpose with the death of their leader, Joshua. Regardless of the excuse, their disobedience and justification for that disobedience came with a great cost—"another generation grew up who knew neither the LORD nor what he had done for Israel."

Let's pause for a moment and allow those words to penetrate our outlook on ministry—just one generation later and the Israelites had already forgotten the Lord and all he had done for them. Not ten, not two, but one!

That is why we say we are just one generation away from the extinction of Christianity. If we as Christian soldiers in children's ministry fail to pass on God's Word to the next generation, it's all over. Please hear me on this: We are not talking about a catastrophic attack from the enemy. All it would take to create a world in which the name of our Lord and Savior Jesus Christ is completely erased from the hearts and lips of this generation is for us to stop trying.

That's what happened with Israel. They failed to pass on the truth of God's Word to the next generation because they were lulled to sleep by the intoxicating fumes of compromise. There was no urgency on their part, allowing the enemy time to draw them into the temporary attractiveness of the sinful lifestyle God was trying to protect them from. The Israelites were given their marching orders, but they felt no urgency and did nothing. It's like what Jesus said in Matthew 25 about the talents, the story I shared in chapter 1. The lazy servant in the parable of talents felt no urgency to invest the money his master left in his care. He simply dug a hole and buried the one talent entrusted to him. Just as it did with the Israelites, the lazy servant's lack of urgency cost him everything—his very life (Matt. 25:26–30).

The Attack from the Gray

Not only did the lazy servant lack urgency, he had no plan. How do we know this? He buried the talents he received from his master—an act requiring no plan and very little effort. I seriously doubt you have literally dug a hole in the ground and buried every opportunity God has given you. However, there are children's ministry leaders all around the world who have a clear, definite calling on their lives, yet they have no thoughtful plan or strategy for the ministry. The absence of strategic thinking and vision creates one of the biggest missed opportunities of them all. It's all too common, and it covertly limits the eternal impact that you were destined to have.

Make no mistake, the enemy is not burying his opportunity in the ground. He is determined to cleverly deceive our children day and night. With as little noise as possible, the enemy attempts to lure our kids away from the truth of God's Word and into a world of compromise that is camouflaged with the tolerance of sin.

There are certainly obvious and overt attacks on our

children from the enemy. And these attacks must be recognized and taken seriously. What frightens me more, however, are the covert attacks—the quiet demons that pursue our children from the gray. These attacks mix in just enough truth with the lies to mask sin with the appearance of righteousness. On a color wheel, if the color black represents sin, and the color white represents truth, it only takes a little of the color black mixed into the color white to create the confusing gray zone. This gray zone is the area that can easily go overlooked by our parents and leaders and is comprised of things we believe are safe for our kids, when in reality they are actually life-threatening poison.

In 2012 a book was published called *The Magic of Reality* by the well-known atheist Richard Dawkins. Dawkins has crafted several well-written works in which he strives to convince his readers that God does not exist. *The Magic of Reality* specifically targets children.[26] I've seen children's coloring books published by satanic cults that concerned me less because the evil and deception in that kind of propaganda can be spotted a mile away. However, a creative, well-produced work that couches its lies within a framework of soothing language? Those attacks are much harder to distinguish. Jesus warns us in Matthew 7:15, "Beware of false prophets who come disguised as harmless sheep but are really vicious wolves" (NLT).

The Scripture warns us to be aware of the crafty tactics of Satan. His strategy is less overt and more covert. The enemy's goal is deception by means of infiltration and assimilation. If the enemy, the vicious wolf named in Matthew 7, can camouflage himself as a harmless sheep, he can gain access to the easily influenced hearts and minds of our children, and he can deceive them through compromise and conformity.

It is becoming increasingly difficult for our kids to distinguish the truth from the lies that hold the appearance of truth. Please hear my heart in this: I don't mean to be depressing or discouraging; rather, I am attempting to splash cold water on all of us to wake us up to the realities of the war we are fighting. Our children are being attacked in ways more strategic than ever. As we partner with parents and rely on the power of the Spirit, we must protect our children and move them toward spiritual health to fully prepare them for the deception of the enemy.

Making the Most of Every Opportunity

I'm going to end this book the same way I began, by asking you this question: Are you making the most of the opportunity God has given you?

> *So be careful how you live. Don't live like fools, but like those who are wise. Make the most of every opportunity in these evil days.*
>
> EPHESIANS 5:15–16 NLT

At this moment, you have an opportunity to change the landscape of eternity. You were designed for this; you were strategically placed for this; you were destined for this. How do I know this? Because you are where God has you. And until that reality changes, do what you can with what you have to move those kids one step closer on their journey toward spiritual health. The conditions will not be perfect, and you will not always have the resources you need. But that is no excuse. We were called and commissioned by the God of the universe, the one who spoke the world into existence and rescued us from despair and misery. He promised to bring us overwhelming victory. And he offers salvation, hope, peace, and joy to the little ones in your care. But the opportunity in front of you will not be there forever. You must fulfill your calling with a sense of urgency.

We must quickly carry out the tasks assigned us by the one who sent us. The night is coming, and then no one can work. But while I am here in the world, I am the light of the world.

JOHN 9:4–5 NLT

If I could look you in the eyes right now and share the most important thing on my heart, it would be this: Stay the course. Don't give up on the calling God has placed on your life to influence the lives of children. Live and lead purposefully and intentionally. And when you fail or things don't go the way you expected, get up and keep moving forward in the divine calling God placed on your life.

The godly may trip seven times, but they will get up again.

PROVERBS 24:16 NLT

We must persevere through the storms, lead with passion, and serve with a kingdom perspective.

I am confident that God will provide the necessary strength, resources, and support for you and your ministry as you progressively move forward with courage and confidence, trusting in God's transformational process, as you lead kids on a journey toward spiritual health.

Remember this—what you do makes an eternal difference.

Every step, big or small, contributes to changing the landscape of eternity.

Jesus made the most of his opportunity when he said, "I brought glory to you here on earth by completing the work you gave me to do" (John 17:4 NLT). The apostle Paul made the most of his opportunity: "I have fought the good fight, I have finished the race, and I have remained faithful" (2 Tim. 4:7 NLT).

What are you doing with your opportunity to change the landscape of eternity?

The clay is drying . . .

Visit www.childrensministryonpurpose.com to download the free discussion guide with reflection questions and activities for the Conclusion. We'll close out our time together by considering several simple but powerful questions that remind us of the urgency and importance of children's ministry.

Acknowledgments

Exodus 17 describes a moment in the life of Moses when he had to embrace the help of others to complete the task God gave him. At different points in the process of writing this book, I felt like Moses when his arms were simply "too tired to hold up the staff any longer." At that point Aaron and Hur came to Moses' side and held up his arms.

There are many people to thank for "holding up my arms." I'm honored and humbled that God would allow me to be a part of a resource like this, and I recognize that I could not have done it without the people in my life supporting me.

I want to thank my wonderful wife, Stephanie, and my sons, Tyler and Matt. Steph, thanks for patiently and gracefully supporting and encouraging me through this challenging season. I know it has not been easy, and you made many sacrifices throughout this process that most people will never be aware of. Thank you for pushing me through the times I was ready to give up. I love you.

Tyler and Matt, you were also an encouragement to me in both big and small ways. I'm proud of you both and appreciate the unique way you "spurred me on." Love you guys.

A special thanks to my pastor, Rick Warren, for trusting me and encouraging me to write this book.

Thanks to Cynthia Petty for leading with such brilliance and always looking for ways to lighten my load. Cynthia, I could not ask God for a more competent and enjoyable second-chair leader to serve alongside.

Thanks to Susan Terry, Joseph Maulorico, Cynthia Petty, Sue Morrow, Becky Downs, and Becky Bernardes for reading this manuscript countless times and providing great input. As busy as you guys are, you were always willing to listen to my ideas and help me work through them. You guys "held up my arms" many times through this process, and I can't thank you enough for that. I could not have done this without you.

A big thanks to the entire Saddleback Kids team for faithfully and effectively carrying out the mission while continually supporting me through this process. You guys are the best team on the planet!

Thanks to Michael Grove for illustrating the MAP. Michael, I appreciate all the hours you put into that beautiful image and patiently working with me on all the changes.

Thanks to my parents, Basil J. Adams and Naomi Adams, for patiently loving and supporting me throughout my life and providing me with an effective framework for ministry. I love you guys.

And thanks to my sisters, Pam, Joy, Faith, and Cheryl. They didn't actually do anything to help with this project, but I said I would mention them.

Notes

1. Rick Warren, *The Purpose Driven Church: Every Church Is Big in God's Eyes* (Grand Rapids, MI: Zondervan, 1995).
2. Francis Chan, *Multiply: Disciples Making Disciples* (Colorado Springs: Cook, 2012), 16.
3. Dallas Willard, *The Great Omission: Reclaiming Jesus's Essential Teachings on Discipleship* (New York: HarperCollins, 2005), 57.
4. Bob Rosen, *Grounded: How Leaders Stay Rooted in an Uncertain World* (San Francisco: Jossey-Bass, 2014).
5. Warren, *The Purpose Driven Church*, 81.
6. Andy Stanley, *Deep and Wide: Creating Churches Unchurched People Love to Attend* (Grand Rapids, MI: Zondervan, 2016), 287.
7. Warren, *The Purpose Driven Church*, 88–89.
8. Ibid., 76–77.
9. Aubrey Malphurs, *Look Before You Lead: How to Discern and Shape Your Church Culture* (Grand Rapids, MI: Baker, 2013), 20.
10. Robert Lewis and Wayne Cordeiro, *Culture Shift: Transforming Your Church from the Inside* Out (San Francisco: Jossey-Bass, 2005), 3.
11. Doug Fields, *Purpose Driven Youth Ministry: Nine Essential Foundations for Healthy Growth* (Grand Rapids, MI: Zondervan, 2013), 91.
12. Aubrey Malphurs, *Values Driven Leadership: Discovering and Developing Your Core Values for Ministry* (Grand Rapids, MI: Baker, 2004).
13. Don Cousins, *Experiencing LeaderShift: Letting Go of Leadership Heresies* (Colorado Springs: Cook, 2010).

14. J. Oswald Sanders, *Spiritual Leadership: Principles of Excellence for Every Believer* (Chicago: Moody, 2005), 15.

15. John Maxwell, *Everyone Communicates, Few Connect: What the Most Effective People Do Differently* (Nashville: Nelson, 2010), 3.

16. Greg McKeown, *Essentialism: The Disciplined Pursuit of Less* (New York: Crown, 2014), 48.

17. Liz Wiseman, *Multipliers: How the Best Leaders Make Everyone Smarter* (New York: HarperCollins, 2010), 11.

18. Ken Blanchard and Phil Hodges, *Lead Like Jesus: Lessons from the Greatest Leadership Role Model of All Time* (Nashville: Nelson, 2005), 3–4.

19. "Microsoft Attention Spans," *Attention Spans* (Consumer Insights, Microsoft Canada), https://advertising.microsoft.com/en/wwdocs/user/display/cl/researchreport/31966/en/microsoft-attention-spans-research-report.pdf.

20. Stan Guthrie, *All That Jesus Asks: How His Questions Can Teach and Transform Us* (Grand Rapids, MI: Baker, 2010), 18.

21. J. Stewart Black and Hal B. Gregersen, *Leading Strategic Change: Breaking Through the Brain Barrier* (Upper Saddle River, NJ: Prentice Hall, 2003).

22. Peter Greer and Chris Horst, *Mission Drift: The Unspoken Crisis Facing Leaders, Charities, and Churches* (Bloomington, MN: Bethany, 2014), 20.

23. Viktor Frankl, *Man's Search for Meaning* (Boston: Beacon, 2006).

24. Mihaly Csikszentmihalyi, *Flow: The Psychology of Optimal Experience* (New York: HarperCollins, 1991).

25. Bill Hybels, *Holy Discontent: Fueling the Fire That Ignites Personal Vision* (Grand Rapids, MI: Zondervan, 2007), 27.

26. Richard Dawkins, *The Magic of Reality: How We Know What's Really True* (New York: Free Press, 2012).